FILL YOUR CUP
DAILY

Practical Self-Care Strategies for a Happy and Fulfilling Life

DEBORAH ARMSTRONG BRYANT

Higher Ground Books & Media
P.O. Box 2914
Springfield, OH 45501-2914
www.highergroundbooksandmedia.com
1-937-970-0554

Because of the dynamic nature of the Internet, any web addresses or links contained in this
book may have changed since publication and may no longer be valid. The views expressed
in the work are solely those of the author and do not necessarily reflect the views of the
publisher, and the publisher hereby disclaims any responsibility for them.

Any people depicted in stock imagery are being used for illustrative purposes only.

ISBN (Paperback): 978-1-955368-23-0

Printed in the United States of America 2022

FILL YOUR CUP DAILY

Practical Self-Care Strategies for a Happy and Fulfilling Life

DEBORAH ARMSTRONG BRYANT

Table of Contents

People all Around
Difficult People

SELF-CARE IN THE LIVES OF OTHERS

REFLECTION & CONCLUSION

INTRODUCTION

If you are reading these pages now, I hope you have decided that it is finally *time*...time to stop feeling exhausted, stressed, drained, and overwhelmed. It is time to stop putting everyone and everything in front of your own self-care because ultimately, you can't fully give to others if you are depleted. I hope you have decided that now is the time to find inner peace, discover lasting joy, and feel the fulfillment in your life that you deserve. There is no better time than the present to reconnect with the deepest part of yourself and feel whole again. It is my deepest desire that this book will bring you comfort in knowing that you are not alone in your journey and that you are fully worthy and deserving of living a happy and fulfilling life. I hope that you will feel inspired by the ideas on these pages and begin to incorporate your favorite self-care practices into your own life on a regular basis in order to enhance your enjoyment of each and every day. I am here to testify that it works.

Although I have two master's degrees and have written plenty of research papers complete with evidence, facts, and citations to back up my theses, that is *not* what I intend to do here. There are plenty of books and studies out there about the harmful effects of compassion fatigue and stress as well as the benefits of mindfulness, meditation, and healthy choices for physical and mental wellbeing. As a school counselor who is passionate about these subjects, I have spent years reading about and studying these topics as well as attending countless workshops and professional trainings. The facts are out there in abundance. What I have to offer is an eclectic understanding of personal development coupled with a desire to support others in living their happiest and most fulfilling lives. Rather than simply citing facts, I am writing from the heart, sharing what I have learned on my journey, what I have found to work for me, and what others have shared with me about their own paths to wellbeing. Take whatever resonates with you and incorporate it into your life, for each and every one of us deserves to experience inner peace and happiness.

I am grateful to be able to say that most of the time I feel happy. I have a lust for life and an appreciation for the simplest of things. I don't necessarily need adventure to entertain me (though it can surely be fun) because I am completely entertained, charged, and thoroughly satisfied with observing, appreciating, and enjoying all of the simple yet beautiful aspects of life, nature, family, and love. I don't understand boredom at all, as I can't see myself ever running out of things I am inspired to do. To list a few: I love to read, write, garden, create in my kitchen, do various projects in my home, engage in meaningful conversations, and bask daily in nature's astounding beauty...the list goes on and on. I absolutely love my life and feel blessed beyond belief. Although this is my experience now, this has not always been the case. It has been a long journey to get to where I am currently. I have learned so much along the way, and at this stage in my life I feel compelled to share what I have learned in the hopes of inspiring others to see life through a new lens, and in turn, create the inner happiness that we all innately desire.

I have experienced my share of trials and tribulations along with many inner emotional struggles during my younger years. I evolved into a woman who overworked, over-extended, and gave of myself until I felt depleted. In hindsight, I don't think I really understood my own worth. I didn't know how to set healthy boundaries in relationships and also in life. To share just one of many examples, I used to go to work early and stay late on a regular basis only to continually feel like I could never get caught up. Although my scheduled work days are Monday through Friday, I also used to go to work on Saturdays around 6:00 AM (while my family was sleeping) and work for at least four hours. This was my attempt at catching up on things that had piled up during the week. Do you know what I found? It didn't matter how much extra time I put in. I never felt caught up. The inbox continually filled up with more to be done. The more I scrambled to catch up, the more new stuff arrived that needed my attention, almost like a vacuum effect. I was in a hamster wheel with no end in sight.

Now, having come so far, it breaks my heart when I see others doing the same thing to themselves, especially when I see the toll it is taking on them. Some are suffering physically, some are suffering mentally and emotionally, and some are impatiently snapping at the very ones they love and then feeling horrible for having done so. Some have simply burned out on what was once their life's passion. The "givers" of our world and those living with compassion fatigue are my inspiration for writing this book because they need to stay whole and healthy physically and emotionally in order to sustain the ability to assist others. Parents, teachers, health care providers, counselors, deep thinkers, artists, empaths, and humans in general…the need is real and the time is now to implement changes for improvement. We all need and deserve to experience peace, comfort, and joy in our daily lives; and incorporating regular self-care is a huge step in this direction.

Through the years I have discovered many things that I never understood before. By learning to set healthy boundaries, I have grown a thousandfold. My relationships are better, and I love the variety of people in my life. Through learning to set boundaries regarding my time devoted to tasks, I have achieved what I consider to be miraculous results. My workday no longer consumes most of my waking hours, and I find that I get no less accomplished than when I was abusing myself by working six or seven days a week and giving up way too much sleep and family time. As a matter of fact, I actually feel that I am more productive at work now than I ever was when I let it consume my life and drain my energy.

I am currently a school counselor, and I love what I do. I feel so pumped up and energized when I am able to provide help and support to youth and their families. It is emotionally rewarding to be able to make a positive impact on people's lives! I am also a former singer-songwriter whose mom-duties inadvertently squashed my creative muse for years. I do still teach piano lessons, and in doing so, I enjoy the same uplifting feeling that counseling gives me as I work with students one-on-one. What I find interesting though is this: while in the moment of teaching, counseling, mothering, and/or helping someone in some way, I feel energized and fulfilled. However, when the day is done, I realize that I am physically and emotionally *drained*. By sharing my energy and expertise for the benefit of others, I have depleted my own. This is not a bad thing at all as long as I maintain balance by remembering to do one thing: replenish my own tank...fill my own cup back up per se....and yes, it is important to do this *daily*. When we make a point of replenishing our own energy through everyday self-care practices, we feel revitalized. This not only benefits our physical, mental, and emotional well-being, it also benefits those who have come to depend on our support and care.

How does one refill their cup daily? Well, that depends, as it can vary for different people. Throughout this book, I will share several strategies that have worked well for me as well as some favorites that have been shared with me by others. There are many self-replenishing practices to choose from, but I will start with something I learned about myself that helps guide me in my own self-care. As I briefly mentioned earlier, after enjoying being around others, or "people-ing" as I like to call it (whether that be teaching, counseling, mothering, working with others, or just plain visiting and socializing) I need to create a balance of quiet and solitude in order to replenish my energy and reground myself. With that being said, although I love and prioritize a good night's sleep, if I don't have the opportunity for solitude during the day, I have been known to "steal" it from the night by getting up ridiculously early in the morning, staying up later than desired, or even getting up in the middle of the night for a bit. On one such occasion, I got up in the middle of the night, went downstairs, picked up a pen, and just wrote freely. This is something I used to do regularly before I

12

became submerged in the many joys and tasks of motherhood. I share this personal experience and poem as an example of reconnecting with one's soul, for on this particular night, I felt that I did just that. I hope you enjoy as I let you peek into my thoughts and heart through this poem.

Between Night and Day

Stealing away time...
Me time...
Just the ticking of the clock...and me
To read?
To write?
It feels so good to just be...
To just BE...
To think...
To exist in the beautiful quiet...
To reside in my mind
So blissfully...
So blessed!

My "Lucky" dog gets up too...
To BE with me...
My children are thriving...
I am blessed...
My daughter, so like me...
Is on a quest...
To venture out and blossom
To create
And be inspired!

"Too blessed to be stressed" takes on such a deep
meaning
At this peaceful hour
Of life contemplation...

It has come full circle!
My daughter is the embellishment...
The evolvement...
Of me...
Yet she...
Is her *own SHE*...

Life is so beautiful!
I am so blessed!

My heart is full!

My son…
My daughter…
My family…
My love…
My doggie…
We are all on such a beautiful path…
So blessed to share it…
With my friends
My "people"
Both near and far…

I am so blessed…
And now here I am…
Writing again!

Yes, life has come full circle…
My daughter…
Oh, never mind
Let me instead plan Easter dinner's menu…
That will be much less complicated…

So here I am
Writing again
Freely
My muse has been unleashed!
And I feel blessed

What is an epiphany?
Because I feel like I just had one!
Crying tears of joy
And gratitude

This hour is so priceless…
This precious time between night & day…

This poem is an example of some free-flowing thoughts that passed through my mind when I was in particular need of some solitude. It was not written with the intention of sharing, but rather a need to express, process, and simply flow with my feelings, thoughts, and emotions in the moment. It was a personal experience that helped me to re-connect with my soul in a way that I used to do often as a young woman when I was responsible for no one but myself. Parts of it were deep, and parts of it were humorous as I freely wrote down my thoughts for the sole purpose of allowing them to flow through me. It felt so good to do so that I was even moved to tears of emotion and gratitude. I share this poem as an example of freewriting, and I invite you to try this process yourself if you feel so inclined. Just grab a pen and paper, get quiet within yourself, and see what flows naturally. The key is...no self-judgment. Write freely, or simply sit and allow yourself to BE. It can truly be a beautiful and personal moment.

Chapter One

SELF-CARE 101

Why is Self-Care so Important?

Do you tend to put yourself last on your priority list? Many of us do, unfortunately. The problem with doing this, however, is that it doesn't just negatively impact you, it also negatively impacts those who rely on you. If you don't keep your own cup full, you will eventually run dry and have nothing left to give. How can you possibly provide quality for others (whether via caregiving or being productive in your passion), if you have not first taken care of yourself? If you have neglected your own self-care you will not be at your best, and this is not fair to those who love, need, and count on you. It is important to make time for self-care daily so that you are whole, healthy, and able to share your personal gifts with the world, especially those nearest and dearest to you. Just like the airlines stress the importance of putting on your own oxygen mask first before assisting others, it is equally essential to take care of yourself as much as you take care of others. This is not selfish; it is healthy. Prioritizing self-care helps maintain balance and can make a difference in the quality of your life in both the short term and the long term.

As I observe the world around me, I see such beautiful and loving people burning out. So many are stressed, sacrificing their own mental and emotional well-being to fulfill whatever role they feel is their purpose. Doing this can lead to feelings of anxiety and/or depression, and often manifests in the form of physical ailments as well. Kind and patient people who don't take care of themselves can end up accidentally taking out their stress and frustration on those very people that they love and care about the most. This can take the form of parents snapping at their kids, parents and spouses not being emotionally available for their family, teachers and caregivers losing their passion for what they do, etc. If someone becomes physically ill due to stress and/or not taking proper care of themselves, they become unavailable to those who need them. Is this the version of us that our children, family, friends, loved ones, clients, patients, or students deserve? Of course not. They (and we) deserve the best version of us, and self-care is paramount to making this happen.

When you were growing up, someone else was responsible for taking care of you. Regardless of whether you think they did a wonderful job or a terrible job, it is no longer their job. It is now yours. It is now your responsibility to be your own parent and take care of yourself. I believe that most people's innate tendency is to treat others with compassion and kindness, especially when they see someone who is struggling. However, many of us don't automatically give this same compassion and kindness to ourselves. It saddens me that so many of us are guilty of this, and I am passionate about teaching people to treat themselves as well as they would treat someone they love or someone for whom they feel compassion.

During my experiences as a middle school counselor, I recall one time working with a student who was on what I call a "hamster wheel" of negative self-affirmations. After making a poor choice and getting in trouble, he was crying and repeatedly saying statements such as *I'm so stupid, I always mess things up*, etc., to the point where he was seemingly unable to hear anything I had to say to him. He was so focused on his negative self-talk that he was unresponsive to any words I offered him. My first thought was *I need to break him out of this cycle* because it was clear that while he was in this state he was having none of what I had to offer. My instinct told me that we needed to do something physical to *snap him out of it* per se, so I made up a game where we tossed a stress ball back and forth in my office. When he caught the ball it was his turn to speak, and he could have alternating turns of venting his negative feelings with turns for sharing a *positive* in his life or something for which he was grateful. To my luck and surprise, it worked like magic. His positives were so well spoken that I wrote them down for him (at his request) so that he could look back on them during future difficult times. Even his turns for venting became more problem-solving in nature as we progressed through the game.

Somewhere during this session, I asked this student what he would say to someone his age or younger who was feeling discouraged and down on themselves, and his words were authentic and noteworthy. With his tiny eleven-year-old voice he told me what he would say to someone who was struggling, "Don't worry. We all have those days." It was such a precious and compassionate statement to hear. I'm not sure where this phrase comes from, but *from the mouths of babes* was what came to my mind, and his empathetic and encouraging statement ended up on the list of "positives" that we made so he could read them later for his own encouragement. My wish for this little guy on that day is what I wish for all of us now, to treat ourselves with the same compassion that we instinctively give to others.

This brings me to a subject that I feel is paramount to healthy self-care: how we care for ourselves through our continuous thoughts and self-talk.

Self-Care with Words

When you were a baby and young child, it was your caregiver's job to build your self-esteem and confidence with positive statements of encouragement. As with all types of self-care, encouraging and supporting yourself with your thoughts and words is now your own responsibility. If your childhood caregiver(s) did a good job supporting you with words of acceptance and encouragement, you have a great example to follow as you care for yourself in a similar manner. If they did not set a good example, then it's your job now as an adult (and your own current primary caregiver) to complete whatever process you must do to let their treatment of you dissolve into the distant past and begin to treat yourself *now* and *daily* the way you deserve to be treated.

How you talk to yourself internally throughout your day has a tremendous impact on your self-esteem, your self-confidence, and your productivity level. No one can thrive when the words in their own head (or from someone important in their life) are negative and discouraging.

Do you tend to mentally or verbally beat yourself up with criticism, or are your inner thoughts primarily kind, gentle, and encouraging? Think about this: if you spoke to others the same way you "speak" to yourself, would people like you? Would they feel good being around you? If the answer is no, perhaps you should strive for an adjustment.

How do you mentally speak to yourself regarding how you look, how you learn, when you make a mistake, or when you're feeling tired or frustrated? Now compare this to how you would speak to others regarding these same things. Unfortunately, many of us are kinder with the words we speak to others than we are with the words we speak to ourselves through our thoughts. Why? Perhaps it's a multitude of reasons: what we were taught or how we were treated as children, influences from society, and/or the perceived nobleness associated with self-sacrifice and putting one's self last. Regardless of these and perhaps other reasons, negative self-talk is counter-productive to healthy self-esteem and emotional wellbeing. Therefore, as you go through your daily experiences, I urge you to be as kind and encouraging to yourself with your inner thoughts and self-talk as you would be with your words to someone you are supporting. No one can take care of you internally as well as you can, so make it a point to be as compassionate with yourself as you would be with someone you love. Thoughts and words are powerful, and your subconscious absorbs them all. Speak and think into existence that which you want to be true in your own life, and when you hit a bump in the road, just remember the voice of that eleven-year-old boy, "Don't worry…We all have those days."

*The Holistic Effects of Caring for Your Mental and
Emotional Well-Being*

Essentially this whole book is about caring for your
mental and emotional well-being, as the many various self-
care practices have a natural tendency to overlap. When
we care for ourselves physically, we are also tending to our
emotional well-being, for when we feel good physically, we
usually feel better about ourselves emotionally as well.
When we practice compassion and kindness towards
ourselves, our mental well-being is naturally improved.
When our mental state is elevated, our physical state often
follows suit and vice versa. We are deep beings with many
levels, and everything within us is connected. Mind, body,
and spirit are forever intertwined, each reacting to and
affecting the other.

As I reflect on the powerful connection between our
inner thoughts and feelings and our bodies' physical
reaction to them, I am reminded of a fascinating test called
The Muscle Test. This is a simple yet amazing experiment
that can demonstrate the power that thoughts and
emotions have over our physical experience. I believe it
was first introduced to me during my training in
hypnotherapy and the power of the subconscious mind,
and I have since been exposed to it through my own
personal reading and studies. Apparently, it has been
used in holistic medical practice and research for many
years and has the fancy name of applied kinesiology. For
my purposes, I prefer to call it a muscle test, and it clearly
demonstrates the power that our thoughts can have over
our physical sensations and strength. Basically, if
something impacts you mentally or emotionally that is
either not true or not in alignment with your body's natural
balance, your muscles will temporarily "short circuit,"
resulting in a temporary reduction in muscle strength.

There are a few ways to conduct this test, and I will
share two. The first is with two people. One person
stands with their straight arm directly out to the side at
shoulder height. The other person places two fingers on

the wrist of the extended arm and attempts to push the arm down while the other person attempts to keep it where it is. This is a way to get a baseline of their muscle strength. Next, the person holding their arm up focuses on something that they consider to be negative or bad such as hate, war, anger, etc. This is often coupled with repeated verbal statements such as *hate, hate, hate, war, war, war* while also visualizing the negative picture in their mind. While the person is doing this, the other person repeats the attempt at pushing their arm down with two fingers. It is astounding to see how muscle strength and resistance are much weaker while the person is stating, visualizing, and imagining something negative. Next, the opposite is done, where the person focuses on something positive such as love and pictures loving things in their mind while repeating some positive words or statements such as *love, love, love*. Magically, the muscle strength is restored. Try it with a friend and see for yourself.

Another way this test can be conducted is with a sway test, and this particular test can be administered alone. To do this, stand up straight, place your hands on your abdomen, and get a sense of your natural balance. Next, think about, visualize, and say out loud a negative statement such as described above; you can even close your eyes while doing so. Be aware of your balance as you do this. After testing the negative thoughts and statements, repeat the test with the positive thoughts and statements, and again, notice your balance. What tends to happen is that with the negative statements the body's natural balance leans slightly back, and with the positive statements, the body's natural balance leans slightly forward.

I have also seen both of these tests done with speaking a truth vs. a lie. An example would be to repeatedly say what your name is for the truth portion. For the lie portion, you say an obvious lie about yourself such as *I am 20 feet tall* or *my name is* _____ (and insert a name that is not yours). I did the sway test with both the truth vs. lie and then the positive vs. negative and found the results to be astounding, especially with the positive vs. negative test. I definitely noticed a balance shift with the truth vs. lie, but when I got to the part where I was verbalizing and visualizing war, hate, and harm to each other, I was knocked off my balance so much that I had to step backward. I was shocked that the impact was so immense, but it got me thinking about other times I have observed or experienced this myself. Have you ever had a piece of negative news shared with you that made your knees buckle and force you to sit down? I have observed people at a funeral so overcome with grief that they literally collapse or "fall out" as some might say. It is a sad thing to think about, but it is a powerful example of the impact that thoughts and emotions can have on our physical bodies. If negative thoughts can have such a dramatic and immediate effect on our muscles, just imagine the long-term effects that chronic negative thinking could have on one's physical well-being. This concept makes me want to check, monitor, and choose my habitual thoughts very carefully. How about you?

Next, let's take a moment to think about our breath. Breath is essential to life. All day and night 24/7 your body breathes for you, keeping you alive. You don't need to think about it or make it happen. It is a natural life force within you. When we exercise we need more oxygen, so our breathing naturally speeds up. When we are calm or sleeping, our breathing naturally slows down. It is quite miraculous when you think about it. Breathing can also be used as a powerful tool for grounding oneself and relaxing the body and mind. Throughout the day I encourage you to periodically take moments to slow yourself down and do nothing but focus on your breath. This is a wonderful strategy for taking care of yourself and maintaining a form of control over your day rather than allowing it to drag you around like a lasso being swung by a cowboy. I try to do this several times a day and find that it enhances my daily experience by anchoring a calmness within. Sometimes I will close my eyes, go within, and focus solely on my breathing. Doing this for any set or extended amount of time is one form of meditation, a topic we will discuss later. Sometimes during my day I couple some slow deep breaths with looking out the window and appreciating something I see in nature such as a beautiful tree, a bird on a branch, or a beautiful sky. This always brightens my mood and elevates my emotional state. By taking a few moments here and there to stop what you're doing and focus on your breathing, you will bring a sense of serenity into your everyday tasks and routines.

Another subject I would like to touch upon here is mindfulness. Mindfulness, which is big in the mental health field, encourages one to focus on the here and now and is said to reduce stress and anxiety. By being fully present in the moment, we are not reliving painful events from the past nor are we feeling anxious about the future. It is a way to ground oneself in the now, and like the breath, it can help relax the mind and body. For example, be aware of where you are and what you are experiencing in the moment through all of your senses. Feel the weight of your body in your chair or the feeling of your feet on the ground. What do you currently feel with your hands? What is the texture, the weight, the temperature? When you are eating, be mindful of the visual appearance of the food, its smell, and its texture, in addition to what it tastes like. These are small examples of mindfulness, a widespread practice that is currently very popular in research, psychology, education, and the mental health fields.

With mindfulness being such a widely studied and taught method of self-care, I would be remiss if I didn't mention it here. I encourage you to research more about this topic and enjoy reaping the many benefits it has to offer.

Another powerful tool for not only mental and emotional well-being but also physical well-being is laughter. Ah, the joy of laughter! Aside from the pleasure it brings in the moment, it also has many other benefits. Laughter releases endorphins which are the body's natural *feel-good* chemicals. It also stimulates major organs, releases stress, and can allow you to connect with others. These benefits can have positive long-term effects on physical health and the immune system. That being said, what makes you laugh? Whether it is listening to a comedian, watching funny videos, listening to a baby's belly laugh, watching funny TV shows or movies, or something else entirely, make time for these things regularly in your life; for the old saying really does ring true: laughter is the best medicine.

Lastly in this section, I would like to write about something that one may not expect here: Clothing. Yes, clothing. I feel it is important to include this because how you dress can most certainly affect the way you feel. Getting dressed up can make one feel handsome, beautiful, and/or significant, and can aid in boosting one's confidence. In contrast, casual wear can have its own effect on one's mood.

Usually, the first thing I do when I arrive home from work is take off my work clothes and put on "comfy clothes" as I like to call them. Doing this brings me an immediate sense of physical and emotional comfort, and it is one way that I practice self-care. If I can find something that meets the criteria for work clothing, yet also has that comfy feel, even better. To give an example, I have a pair of slacks that look just like dress pants on the outside. What people don't see is that they have a thin layer of fleece on the inside; so even though I look like I am casually dressed up, I *feel* like I am in my pajamas. I have so much fun with this because I go through my day feeling like I came to work in my jammies, yet no one knows it.

I have some friends who use an online company that provides them with a personal "stylist" based on their body type and clothing preferences. This computer-based stylist selects outfits for them that come in the mail. I love it when these ladies get their deliveries because I have seen such joy in them as they try on their new outfits and model them for each other. They share their comments and opinions and sometimes even trade items if something suits one of them more than the other. It brings them a sense of fellowship and sisterhood as well as a chance to find things that enhance their personal styles and make them feel good about themselves.

I will share one last example regarding the effect that clothing can have on how we feel. Sometimes I work hard physically to accomplish a task, such as yard work or gardening. Although I am fully invested while I am doing it, when I finish I am usually sweaty and covered in dirt, mulch, or and/or pollen. After I shower and get all cleaned up, I often like to put on something flowy and feminine such as a comfortable sundress. After working hard and getting dirty, I regain my balance by wearing something that makes me feel pretty and reconnects me with my feminine essence.

What do you like to wear at different times in your day and life, and how does your clothing choice affect your mood? It is amazing how seemingly minor decisions can affect our frame of mind. Having an awareness of this grants us the power to influence how we feel.

Physical Health

It cannot be denied that physical health is important. It not only increases the likelihood of a longer life, it greatly affects the quality of life we experience. While numerous books have been written on this subject with multiple ideas, suggestions, and opinions, I will stick to a few basic principles: Diet, Exercise, and Sleep.

Let me preface this by saying that I am not a health professional. I am simply a layman sharing my personal thoughts and experiences. Without promoting any particular diet or eating style, I will share what has worked for me. I try to eat mostly healthy foods, consume the more indulgent ones in moderation, and drink plenty of water. I enjoy eating natural foods that come from the earth and make an effort to stay away from the more processed foods because I believe this is the healthiest choice. I enjoy buying, growing, handling, and prepping fresh produce because it makes me feel connected to nature in the same way that gardening does. It feels grounding to me, and when I am prepping natural foods I am in my happy place (well, one of them, as there are several). That being said, I am also human and have been known to have a late-night craving resulting in an indulgence of cheesy crackers or some other salty snack. While I savor it in the moment, I usually regret it in the morning. Still, I forgive myself with a reminder for next time, *No late-night snacking Deb;* then I try to do better in the future. I find humor in these occasional weaknesses and try not to let myself stress about them.

Although I certainly can't prove it, I believe that one's thoughts and beliefs about what they are eating can have some influence on the way the body processes the food. After all, humans are complex beings consisting of mind, body, and spirit intertwined. That being said, it just makes sense that if someone is eating something, feeling terrible about it, and feeling like it is going to make them fat or unhealthy, it's probably not a great food choice for them at that moment. However, someone else eating the same thing while feeling like it's fuel for their body or that they have a super-fast metabolism…well, they may experience a different result altogether. Look at those who are overweight yet eat very little, claiming that if they look at food it goes straight to their hips. Then look at people who are thin and enjoy eating anything and everything they want without a care in the world. These examples are everywhere. It is because of the interconnectedness of mind, body, and spirit that I believe our thoughts, beliefs, and emotions can have an impact on how food affects our bodies.

I have read in multiple places that it is never a good idea to eat mindlessly or while stressed as it can negatively affect digestion and/or lead to an overconsumption of food. Although I am not always successful, I make an attempt not to eat while working if at all possible. Instead, I encourage myself as well as you to be more mindful about meal times. I recommend setting aside a period of time during your day, taking a couple of deep breaths to relax, and then thinking about how your food will nourish your body. Taking a break from your daily tasks to enjoy the pleasure of a meal provides an opportunity to rejuvenate yourself both mentally and physically.

In many cultures, mealtimes are considered a gathering time for socializing and bringing together loved ones. Holidays often center around a special meal that includes traditional foods to be enjoyed with family and friends. One tradition that many follow is saying a blessing before a meal. This encourages us to pause for a moment before eating in order to focus on gratitude for the meal as well as other positives in our lives. These traditions are no accident. They expand the importance of mealtimes from solely physical nourishment, to include social and emotional benefits.

Make mealtimes special. Feel appreciation for your food, your blessings, and whoever may be in your presence. This may include merely yourself and your thoughts, or it may expand to include company and conversation enjoyed with others. Bon appetit.

I am going to take a moment here to share a fun little saying that one of my girlfriends and I often use: *Is it calorie-worthy?* What does this mean exactly? Let me preface by mentioning that we basically get a certain number of calories to eat or "spend" in a day, and we get to choose how we spend these calories. Just as we choose what we will spend our money on when creating a budget, we do the same with our food choices every day. As I have said before, the foods that typically dominate my diet are mostly healthy choices. However, sometimes when presented with food that is rarely available, or is just *so* amazingly scrumptious, I will often deem this food to be "calorie-worthy." That means that I purposely don't think about the calories in the food. Instead, I simply enjoy the experience of tasting it fully because the joy and pleasure of eating it are totally worth it. Perhaps I may skip something else in my diet that day to help offset my indulgence, but if it's calorie-worthy, I allow myself to enjoy it guilt-free.

One example of *calorie-worthy* food that comes to mind has occurred during work conferences that include a nice lunch or meal. Often there will be a fancy dessert table with little gourmet treats. Sampling a few of these is something that I consider to be calorie-worthy. I have so much fun picking out and tasting a few from the beautiful display. They are small and not too filling, something I rarely have access to, super delicious, and thus "calorie-worthy." Another example that comes to mind is a piece of cake made by a friend of mine who has a baking talent that he rarely shares. The first time I tried one of his cakes, I jokingly told him it felt like there was a *party in my mouth*. It's funny that I would even say this because I usually am not a cake person at all. Cake just doesn't bring me enough culinary pleasure to justify consuming the empty calories, so I generally don't eat it. However, when this particular friend makes one of his special-occasion cakes, it's like a fine wine; the flavors are exquisite and complex. The way the icing compliments the incredibly moist cake is perfection, and the subtleties and elegance of flavors are simply brilliant. Recently he shared one of his famous cake creations. I happily indulged in the rare opportunity and felt absolutely no guilt for having cake for dinner that night; it was *that* filling as well as sensually gratifying.

There are many foods I might get offered that are considered treats, but to me, they are simply not calorie-worthy. For example, I was offered a piece of a soft pretzel recently while attending an event. Had I been starving, it may have appeared appetizing to me. However, since that wasn't the case, I turned down the kind offer. I was then asked if I dislike soft pretzels. Although I do not dislike them per se, they're fine for what they are; I simply do not get enough culinary enjoyment from that particular food to make it worth consuming the calories they contain. That would be eating empty calories for no reason. If the joy I get from eating something isn't worth the calories I am "spending" to eat it, then it's not calorie-worthy. For something to be worthy of the calories, it must be rare or special or so incredibly tasty that it earns the "calorie-worthy" title and therefore is consumed guilt-free. While I can't speak from the perspective of a dietician or a health coach, I *can* say that I have had fun with this; and one thing I have embraced at my age is that I get to make my own rules for my own life choices. If you are someone who makes an effort to eat mostly healthy foods, do you too have a calorie-worthy exception that you allow yourself to indulge in guilt-free on occasion? If so, cheers to breaking your own rules once in a while!

I would now like to share a few words about exercise. I have exercised to one extent or another for many years, and I believe this has been my fountain of youth. I have been told for years by many different people that they thought I was much younger than I actually am. I am always happy to hear this, and quite frankly, I really *do* feel youthful. My chronological age is most certainly older than my biological age, and I attribute this primarily to two things, attitude and exercise. I believe that regular exercise, as well as my state of mind, has kept me feeling and looking much younger than my years; and for that I am grateful. There are young people who feel, look, and seem old, and there are chronologically old people who are still thriving mentally and physically. Therefore, I believe that attitude and exercise can greatly affect our youthfulness or lack thereof, and these are things that are usually within our control. I have experienced so many benefits, both physically and mentally, from regular exercise, that I always want to incorporate this into my life in some way, shape, or form. Exercise keeps the body moving. It keeps us feeling younger and healthier than one who does not engage in any physical activity.

What does exercise mean to you personally? Is it something rigorous or something as simple as stretching? It might be a basic walk around the block, or it could be a jog, hike, yoga, or tennis with a friend. It matters not what form of movement you choose because we are all vastly different in age, physical health, and preferences. I do think it needs to be something that you enjoy and that does not overwhelm you; for if it's a huge chore, it will be much more difficult to continue doing long term. I have seen my share of people beginning an extensive, time-consuming workout routine that they abandon in a relatively short period of time. The reality is, many people simply cannot maintain spending three hours a day in the gym on a regular basis, no matter how gung-ho they may have initially felt about it. On the other hand, if it's fifteen or thirty minutes a day, or even an hour for some, there is a much greater likelihood that you will be able to keep it up long term once it becomes a habit. The key is to make it a part of your regular routine. So do it, do it, and do it again. Once you've done it enough times for it to become a habit, it will be much easier to stick with it on a regular basis. Commitment to regular exercise has been a self-care gift I have given myself for many years, and the pay back I have received has been monumental! It has not only benefited my physical health, but also my mental and emotional wellbeing. It's good for my body physically, it's a wonderful form of stress relief, and it makes me feel good about myself in many ways. If you don't already, and with your doctor's stamp of approval of course, I encourage you to contemplate a form of movement you could incorporate into your regular routine. Then, after a month or two of consistency, see how it makes you feel. I think you will be pleased with the results.

Sleep...ah glorious sleep! It feels so good to drift into, and after a good night's sleep, I am always my best self with my clearest mind and happiest heart. Sleep gives both the body and mind time to rest, rejuvenate, heal, and recharge. It is part of the body's natural cycle. Lack of sleep can lead to stress, physical ailments, grumpiness, and a slew of other negative consequences, while good healthy sleep has many physical, mental, and emotional benefits. If one doesn't prioritize the sleep that the body needs, guess what? The body will get it one way or another, even if that is through getting sick and being physically unable to do anything else but rest and sleep. I urge you not to let it come to that. The body will win in the long run, so why not care for it regularly and give it the sleep that it needs so that it can, in turn, be what you need to feel good and live your life?

I know that I am only at my best with adequate sleep. Therefore, I make it a priority in my routine. Am I always successful? Of course not, but when I fall off "the sleep wagon" I immediately feel the consequences and make adjustments accordingly. A good sleep routine is good self-care, and it is my understanding that many struggle in this area, unfortunately. One thing that helps me to transition from the day into a restful night of sleep is how I spend the last hours before bedtime. I am self-aware enough to know that I can't arrive home from somewhere in the evening and go straight to sleep. It's just not going to happen. Instead, I need a winding-down period each evening before heading to bed. Whether I spend it watching a favorite television show, reading, or sitting outside appreciating nature, this time for relaxing is essential to me prior to turning in for the night. It feels like a reward for a day well done. I thoroughly enjoy this segment of my evening, and it's a wonderful way to transition from the busyness of the day into the restfulness of a good night's sleep. Knowing this about myself, I make it a point to build this time into my regular routine.

I also recognize that there are many people who seem to need less sleep at night than I do, and I say *Lucky You*. If that were me, I would relish the extra hours I would have in my day. Whatever your personal sleep needs are, I encourage you to take them into consideration as you plan your days and your schedule. How much sleep do you need to be the best, happiest, and most energized person you can be? Honoring your sleep needs is another way of honoring your health and well-being. Sweet dreams!

A Personal Word about Body Image

I have experienced my body at various weights and sizes as well as the corresponding feelings that go along with them. Therefore, even when I am at my ideal weight, I have compassion and understanding for what it feels like

32

to be dissatisfied with one's body image. I get it; I've been there more than once, and it sucks. No matter your current physical state, it is important to understand and remember that we are all beautiful souls, perfect just as we are at any given time, regardless of our physical appearance; what we should be striving for, first and foremost, is self-love and acceptance.

Take care of your body. Love your body. Our bodies are a gift to us, allowing us to move through and experience life in this physical realm. Strive to keep it at the health and fitness level of your comfort, but also commit to loving it unconditionally through its many ages and stages. Physicality is a fluid thing, but the beauty of who we are inside remains consistent through time.

When I had my second baby, my body didn't bounce back as quickly as I had hoped it would. Even though I may not have thought so at the time, my body was still beautiful because it had just served as a vessel to bring a precious life into this world. One day during this post-pregnancy period, I clearly remember catching a glimpse of myself in the mirror and not recognizing that it was me. I saw a reflection of a physically frumpy person who did not look at all like the person I felt like I was on the inside. That was a rude awakening. I realized then that I desperately desired a congruence between who I felt like I was on the inside and the person I saw when I looked in the mirror.

When I see my own reflection, I want to be able to say to myself, *Yes, that's me right there.* It is important to me to feel good in my own skin because I believe this is the most predominant aspect of body image. Size and shape vary vastly between all of us, and I think that this diversity is a wonderful thing. Your size and shape matter not. If you love your body as it is and feel comfortable in your own skin, then quite frankly, I think you're nailing it!

I recognize and appreciate that anyone can struggle with body image and that it can be quite an emotional challenge. Everyone's personal experience is genuinely important and valuable, and I don't want to discount or minimize anyone's experience. However, because I am a woman, it is naturally easier for me to speak from a woman's perspective on this subject. That being said, please allow me to take a brief moment to speak to my fellow female humans. Ladies, we are all goddesses, beautiful in our own ways, in all of our many shapes and sizes. It is important to embrace our feminine beauty in whatever physical form it displays. The media often portrays an image of the female body that is achieved by a minority of women, leaving many to feel like they don't measure up. But we *do* ladies, we do! We are vital to life and its continued existence, and we are all precious works of art. Among many other things, we bear and raise our children, and we care for and support our families. It is absolutely paramount that we know and appreciate our amazing value. We are all sacred beings, and it is my wish and desire for all women to feel like the goddesses that they are regardless of the current shape of their bodies. All women are beautiful; embrace it ladies! *Namaste.*

In closing about body image, it is important to note that all body types can be beautiful. If your body is supportive of your overall health, then the most important thing is that you are comfortable in your own skin. If you are happy with yourself as you are and at peace with your body, that is a great place to be. However, if you are not pleased with the reflection you see in the mirror, take comfort in knowing that just like life, our bodies are fluid; you have the option to take steps towards making changes at any time. Just know and accept that you are beautiful and perfect right now just as you are, even if your desire is to make adjustments in the future. The key is to love yourself completely throughout the process. Do *you* beautiful souls, *do you!*

Caring for Your Spiritual Well-Being

Spirituality as I will define it here is a connection with the source from which we originate, whether one calls this God, Inner Being, The Universe, The Divine, or a plethora of other names. Connecting with one's spirituality is a deeply grounding, peaceful, and enormously beneficial means of self-care. Whether you access this through prayer, meditation, mindfulness, yoga, or some other means, I encourage you to embrace it fully and make a place for it in your life.

There are many ways to care for your spiritual wellbeing, and you get to decide which one(s) you choose to embrace in your life. Being involved and feeling connected with a public place of worship is a well-known protective factor for mental and emotional health. It provides a sense of community and belonging which can greatly enhance one's life. Other ways to feel spiritually connected include prayer, meditation, and a variety of spiritual rituals. Nature is also something that can be spiritually grounding. Walking outdoors or simply basking in nature's astounding beauty can be extremely therapeutic, bringing comfort and peace to one's day. Feeling your bare feet in the grass, or touching something in nature such as a rock, leaf, or tree are all ways of feeling connected to this beautiful universe we live in. The good news is that there are multiple ways to honor and cherish our spirituality, and we each get to choose the one(s) that resonate the most for us.

I can't help but notice that there are many commonalities among the vast diversity of spiritual practices and world religions. We are all connected somehow in this beautiful world of ours, and there are many paths to Divine Truth. Religions and spiritual practices serve such a wide variety of people and cultures all over the world that it is no wonder there are so many of them. Ultimately though, our spiritual practice is a means of achieving a *Connection* with our deepest Core (that from which we are created or that which is within) which brings us the peace and comfort we innately desire. Whatever your religious or spiritual beliefs, I encourage you to embrace and practice them regularly, and in turn, feel an amazing connection that is like no other and that inspires humanity to emanate pure Love!

Caring for Your Emotional Wellbeing

It is important to pay attention to and be mindful of your emotions, and when you are feeling stressed, focus on self-care. Having the ability to self-nurture is a valuable tool for an emotionally healthy life. Remember, once you are grown, you become your own parent; so be good to yourself by taking care of your emotional wellbeing.

Understand that it is okay not to be okay sometimes, and to give yourself permission to seek help when needed. Talk to a friend, family member, clergyman, or a professional; everyone needs help and support at some point in their life.

If you find that you're running late for something, remind yourself that getting worked up and speeding or driving aggressively won't help. In fact, it could potentially lead to even more problems. If you're going to be late, you're going to be late. Sometimes you just have to surrender to the situation.

Be proactive in your time-management, but at the same time, be realistic with your expectations. If you get in over your head, readjust a timeline or request assistance. Do your best, but also understand that you are human, subject to human error. Be generous with self-forgiveness as needed, recognizing that each moment presents us with an opportunity to begin anew.

Occupational Wellness

How do you spend the majority of your day? Often this is your occupation or employment, but it can also extend to include other activities such as raising your family, attending school and studying, community involvement, or caring for a loved one. Now consider this next question: Does it bring you satisfaction and enjoyment? If it does, that is an ideal way to live. If it does not, I urge you to prioritize creating a balance between your work and your leisure time to assure that you are nurturing yourself. In addition, as you plan for your future, I invite you to consider what would bring meaning and purpose to your life and strive toward making this your reality.

When I went to school to become a teacher, becoming a school counselor would have been my first choice. However, due to the time requirements and financial sacrifices needed to obtain my preferred certification, it was not an option for me at the time. So I embraced my second choice, completed the teaching program, and got the secure job that I needed. Although I taught for many years, I can distinctly remember the exact moment when I knew it was time to finally become a school counselor. I was attending a work seminar, and a teacher was speaking about the reading program with such incredible fervor that it got me thinking. She clearly had a deep love for the academic curriculum, and I recognized that as a teacher I probably should share her enthusiasm. However, the reality was I did not. That realization left me feeling slightly guilty and a little bit like a hypocrite. My passion was not about the curriculum. Instead, it was about the students I got to work with every day who, aside from learning the required subject matter, also needed to learn about mutual respect, conflict resolution, and their own intrinsic value. My passion was about human behavior, youth, and how I could best be of service to them. I knew right then and there that it was time to tend to my occupational wellness by going back to school for counseling and working towards a career that aligned with my passion.

I share this story as an example to demonstrate that the way you spend the majority of your days currently may be changed or adjusted when the time or opportunity presents itself. Strive to enjoy each and every day as much as possible, whether your occupational situation is currently ideal or not. If it is not, keep the vision in mind of what you would prefer and brainstorm paths that could lead you in that direction. In the meantime, try to focus on the most positive aspects of your current situation while also maintaining a healthy balance between fulfilling your obligations and dedicating time to your own self-care.

Financial Wellness

First and foremost, live within your means. Unmanageable debt can be an enormous source of stress. It can negatively impact not only your personal life but also the lives of those you love and/or provide for. It can lead to embarrassment and a temptation to lie. Living with unmanageable debt is like living in a house of cards that could be destroyed at any moment. Financial mismanagement has caused people to lose their homes, their marriages, and their families.

Be aware of your wants, needs, and priorities, and then create a proactive financial plan for how you can most effectively balance and fulfill them, i.e., a budget. A budget is not intended to be viewed as a restriction, but rather as a carefully thought out plan for how you want to spend your money based on your needs, financial goals, and desires, both current and future. A good financial plan can provide a sense of security as well as the blessing of having options, freedoms, and choices. It can also avert the enormous amount of stress that can occur when unexpected costs arise. Making financial wellness a priority in your life is paramount to healthy self-care practice, and its benefits are monumental.

Some Self-Care Ideas & Activities

Self-care activities can vary amongst different people. Think about things that you could do to care for yourself. In no particular order, I have listed some ideas to consider. Read through them and contemplate which ones might bring some joy into your day. Once you select some (or come up with your own), challenge yourself to incorporate them into your life on a more frequent basis.

- <u>Hug someone you love</u>. Doing this can be a huge stress reliever as it releases "feel-good" hormones that naturally help us to feel happier.

- <u>Snuggle or play with a cherished pet.</u> Animals are natural energy balancers and can be very therapeutic. Most people's moods naturally brighten when they interact with a puppy, a dog, or another pet.
- <u>Buy yourself flowers.</u> Put them in a space that you frequent in order to have something beautiful to look at, smell, and appreciate throughout your day. They can also serve as a reminder to stop periodically, breathe in and out mindfully, and simply be present, knowing that all is well.
- <u>Take yourself on a date.</u> Dinner? A movie? A hike? What is it that you enjoy? Well then, get out there and do it. Being someone who enjoys my own company, I love taking myself out to a favorite restaurant once in a while for a little break in my day. When time allows, sometimes I even extend it a bit and enjoy some reading. There have been times when I have stopped at a restaurant on my way home from work simply to provide myself with a few minutes of *me-time* in between the demands of work and home life. The times I have done this I have arrived home mentally refreshed and ready to enter into my domestic world. Think of some things that you like to do for fun and make a point to fit them into your schedule.
- <u>Spend time with a friend.</u> There are many activities that can be enjoyed with a companion. See a movie with a friend, or catch up over a cup of coffee or a meal. Enjoy a hike together or simply a leisurely walk. The activity you choose matters not. Do whatever it is that you both prefer and enjoy. The true value comes from the time spent in each other's company. While solitude can be very useful for recharging, companionship is equally chock-full of benefits. Conversations with someone we enjoy can help us to feel heard and understood. Sharing something with another person can often help us to see a topic from another perspective that perhaps

we hadn't considered. Truly listening with compassion to someone can make us feel valued and appreciated. We naturally give and receive support through our relationships. Whether conversing with someone or simply being present with them in silence, we are social beings who benefit from connecting with others.

- <u>Dance to your favorite music.</u> Dancing is a wonderful form of expression as well as a great stress reliever. It is an activity that can significantly elevate one's entire mood and demeanor. I have been known to dance around my house all by myself simply because it's fun, and a girlfriend of mine and I have often ended a weekend night of hanging out with an impromptu dance session in the living room. I highly recommend it. I have another friend who turned her entire life around by rediscovering her love for music and dancing. When I asked what her secret was regarding how she went from rock bottom to creating a wonderful and successful life, she said it was the energy shift that occurred within her when she reconnected with her favorite music and started attending concerts and dancing again. This energy shift, which resulted from her unbounded joy while dancing, expanded to affect her attitude and ultimately improved the momentum of her life.

- <u>Stretch or do yoga.</u> The practices of stretching and yoga not only have many physical benefits; they are also advantageous to your mental and emotional well-being because they are natural stress relievers. For many, yoga is part of their spiritual practice as well as their physical routine. Whether you decide to take a class or follow along to a video, enjoy knowing that these activities can have holistically positive effects on your overall well-being. *Namaste.*

- <u>Meditate</u>. There are many ways to meditate. One common form is guided meditation. This is where a voice leads a person or group of people through the meditation process. The voice may use guided imagery and visualization to mentally transport the participants to a desirable place, or it may lead them to imagine a healing light traveling gently through the body. Some guided meditations lead the listeners to focus on different parts of the body with the intention of relaxing each one. There are countless meditations to choose from, and they are available in abundance online or through various meditation apps. I have a couple of these on my phone that I use and enjoy regularly. Some even offer a full array of free meditations to educators as an encouragement to utilize meditation in the school setting. I will conclude this section with one other common way to meditate. Simply sit comfortably, close your eyes, and focus only on your breath for a set amount of time, perhaps 15 or 20 minutes, or whatever amount of time you choose. When your mind begins to wander, and it most likely will, don't worry. Just gently bring your focus back to your breath. As many people have attested, meditating on a daily basis can have a profound impact on one's mental and emotional wellness.

- Practice mindfulness frequently throughout your day. As previously discussed, take a deep breath and focus on the here and now. What do you currently see, hear, and feel? How does your body feel in the chair at this moment? If you have a water bottle or a beverage how heavy does it feel? What is the temperature? What is the texture of its container? How does it feel in your mouth, and how does it taste when you drink it? Do you see anything in your view that could be considered beautiful? If so, focus on it for a few moments. What are the qualities that make it beautiful to you? By focusing specifically on the details of what you are experiencing here and now, stress and anxiety about the past or future naturally fall by the wayside.

- Create something in the kitchen. How do you feel about cooking or baking? For some, this can be a wonderful form of self-care. Focusing on a recipe and the task at hand can naturally cause all other thoughts to dissipate, hence relieving stress. Cooking can also be an outlet for expressing one's creativity. I like getting inspired by one or more recipes and then using creative liberty to put my own twist on them. I call it *playing in my kitchen*. I intentionally use the word "playing" so that there's no pressure for me to be a knowledgeable chef. As I stay in the moment and create whatever I am inspired to make, I feel happy. I also enjoy cleaning and prepping natural fruits and vegetables because I find it grounding in a similar way that gardening feels. Whether it be baking, prepping produce, or cooking meals, your level of culinary expertise matters not. If it brings you joy, then partake to your heart's content.
- Sit outside and appreciate. Notice your surroundings and find things that you can admire. This is one of my personal favorites, and I refer to it as *basking*. I absolutely love to stand or sit on my deck and bask in the beauty around me: the trees, the birds, etc. I feel so peaceful and blessed when I do this, so I try to take at least a few minutes every day to go out there for this very purpose. Basking can look however you like. It could be sitting anywhere outside appreciating the view, the fresh air, or the city lights; or it could be sitting on a porch enjoying watching the happenings of the neighborhood. I have even seen neighbors sitting in their garage with the door open for the sole purpose of relishing a good rainstorm. If you can step outside and notice things you like in your environment, you are successfully basking. Try it. It can do wonders for the soul.

- Notice and appreciate the beauty of the ever-changing sky. From the beautiful designs of the morning sunrise, and the various clouds that may appear throughout the day, to the vast array of colors and designs of the evening as the sun gently descends, the sky always seems to have an ever-changing story to tell. Even the presentations it displays associated with an upcoming or recent storm can be breathtaking. Feeling well-rested after a good night's sleep, I admire the early morning sky most days as I drive to work, and it brings me a feeling of joy and peace. When I arrive at work and do my outside morning duty, I enjoy it yet again, so beautiful and always changing as time passes. In an upcoming chapter, I elaborate further on one of my sky-watching episodes. The sky is an aesthetic blessing that is consistently there for us. All we have to do is take the time to notice.

- Plant something. Have you thought about trying out your green thumb? Whether it be a potted plant, a flower, or an outdoor garden of any size, getting your hands in the dirt and watching something grow can be therapeutic as well as rewarding. A friend of mine shared with me that he loves working in his yard because he doesn't think about anything else but the task at hand. In turn, he experiences relief from any stressful thoughts. This can be a form of mindfulness, complete with its many benefits. Another friend who had been spending most of her recent time gardening, shared her surprise and delight when she noticed many other things in her life effortlessly working out for her. She concluded that by focusing on and participating in something she loved, the positive energy and attitude she emanated had expanded into other areas of her life. Gardening can help you to feel grounded (no pun intended), and a trip to a garden center in the springtime is ample evidence that there are many who agree.

- Fix or treat yourself to a fancy cup of coffee or other drink of choice. Whether it be a coffee break, a drink with a friend, a toast to a special occasion, an iced tea on a hot summer's day, or a hot beverage to stay warm in the winter, there is something to be said about the enjoyment of pouring ourselves a drink once in a while. This brings me back to happy childhood memories of drinking hot cocoa after playing in the snow and the warm, fuzzy feeling it would give me inside. Many years later I enjoyed preparing the same for my own kids when they would come in cold and wet from building a snowman. Another beverage ritual that comes to mind is when my daughter and I have what we call "movie mornings" when we agree to get up early on a weekend to watch a movie together. In preparation for these mother-daughter events, I always prepare us each a hot and fancy drink, whether it be hot chocolate with marshmallows or a flavored coffee beverage topped with whipped cream and a dash of cinnamon. It feels so good to curl up in our favorite seats, press "play," and sip our morning comfort drinks. Do you have any beverage rituals of your own that you associate with special moments or self-care? Perhaps a fine wine with a special meal or a cup of hot tea before bed? Or the natural simplicity of a clear glass of water to rejuvenate the body and mind. You could even make it resemble a spa refreshment by adding lemon, cucumber, or strawberries. The possibilities are endless. Treat yourself well, create and treasure special moments, and remember that life's simplest pleasures can provide the greatest joy and happiest memories.
- Take a walk outside. Getting outside is such a healthy thing to do. Breathe in the fresh air and take in the sights. Although walking in nature is always a treat, sometimes a simple walk around the neighborhood can be just as pleasurable. I enjoy

taking my dog with me when I do this, and I often get a chance to greet a neighbor or two in the process which adds a nice bonus. There are some that use walking as a form of meditation, focusing the mind only on the process of walking. Others like to listen to something with headphones, take in the sights, or engage in conversation with their walking companion(s). However one chooses to enjoy walking, it is not only great for the body, it is also good for the soul.

- Pamper yourself by having a leisurely soak in the tub. Feel free to make it extra special by adding candles, your favorite music, and a cup of herbal tea, a glass of water, or another beverage of choice. Soak, relax, and enjoy. You deserve it!

- Watch or listen to something that makes you laugh. Whether it be sitcoms, funny movies, stand-up comedy, or funny video clips, find something that makes you laugh and enjoy the experience. I have gotten many belly-laughs watching funny TV shows with my family, and I sometimes enjoy listening to comedians while I drive or get ready for work. Find what makes you laugh, and experience the many aforementioned benefits of laughter.

- Read something that interests you. Ah, the many joys of reading! I love to read a good fiction novel and escape with my mind into the story. It can be both relaxing and captivating at the same time. I also love to read inspirational books and quotes because they feed my positive attitude and make me feel good inside. Reading is also a terrific way to care for your intellectual wellness by exercising your mind, enhancing your personal development, and learning something new.

- List things you love about yourself. What are your positive attributes? When you assess your character and accomplishments in life, what makes you feel most proud? Most of us could easily highlight someone else's positive qualities and successes in order to uplift and encourage them. I challenge you to do the same for yourself.

- Save your kudos. When someone thanks you or recognizes you in a positive way, own it and cherish it. I have a folder in my email that I have labeled "Kudos." When someone emails me a thank you, an appreciation, or a recognition for a job well done, I file it in my *Kudos* folder to be reread whenever I need a pick me up or a reminder of my value to others. Display accomplishments that you are proud of such as awards, trophies, diplomas, and certificates, and let them be visual reminders of what you have achieved. I recently noticed a bulletin board in a local business that displays notes and reviews from happy customers. What a creative way to keep morale high in a work environment by showcasing the positive effect the employees are making on their customers. Embrace your kudos and use them to remind yourself of your accomplishments and the positive impact you have on the world.

- Text or call a loved one. Although I am an introvert who absolutely needs and loves her solitude, I also value my connection with my family and close friends. My day always feels more fulfilled when I have been able to have a phone chat or text (whichever is our preferred method of communication) with a family member. That connection makes me feel whole and complete. Who in your life makes you feel good when you connect with them? Go ahead, reach out if you feel so inclined.

- Tap into your creative side with a little art therapy. Drawing, painting, and coloring are known to be great stress relievers. Any type of arts and crafts can help us to focus our attention on the task at hand while forgetting about the tensions of daily life. Adult coloring is quite popular these days, and there is a wide array of adult coloring books available. I have a few friends who enjoy coloring medallions. This can be a calming activity which can also be used as a form of meditation. Perhaps you could enhance your artistic time with your favorite music. Enjoy knowing that this is time you are dedicating to yourself. On a more social scale, why not schedule a paint night? These have become quite popular and are a great way to bond with friends while connecting with your inner artist.

- Learn to play an instrument. Music is not only therapeutic, it's a great way to express your creativity. I have never once heard anyone say, "I am glad that I quit piano lessons when I was a kid." In fact, quite the opposite. If I had a dollar for every time someone told me they wish they'd never quit, I would have quite a large pile of money. The good news is that it's never too late. So why not? Learning to play an instrument is a fun way to keep the mind active while also experiencing many additional benefits such as increased coordination, discipline, concentration, and patience.

- Watch a favorite show or movie. Growing up I was always involved in musical and theatrical performances which kept me out many evenings at rehearsals and shows. I distinctly remember one night picking up someone from their home for a rehearsal and noticing their family all snuggled around in their family room watching a show together. They looked so cozy and happy. At the time I was content to be out doing my music, but the memory of that family scene has stuck with me to this day. Having lived so many years out and about at night pursuing my musical endeavors, I now have a full appreciation for the contrasting coziness of a relaxing night at home. After years of minimal to no television, I cherish evenings of curling up on the couch and decompressing to a favorite show or movie. I chuckle as I reflect on being teased by dear ones for some of my movie choices. I can laugh at myself too as these shows are admittedly quite predictable with their repeated actors and recurring plots. Even so, they make me feel warm and fuzzy inside because the characters are all attractive, happy, and frequently smiling. The houses they take place in are gorgeous, and I love seeing all of the beautifully decorated rooms. The experience is comparable to flipping through a magazine and marveling at the lovely homes and decorations. Add a bowl of popcorn, and I'm in another one of my happy places. Whatever your viewing pleasure, taking the time to watch something you enjoy either alone or with others can be a form of self-care.

- Read and share uplifting quotes and affirmations. Put them in places that you frequent, for they can be great reminders and pick-me-ups throughout your day. I enjoy surrounding myself with them for this very reason. At work, I have quotes placed in subtle locations for myself affirming my effectiveness and fulfillment in my job. On the walls of my office for those who come to see me are various uplifting pictures and inspirational sayings. As I enter my home through my garage door, I have a quote posted on the door reminding me that my home welcomes me with warmth and comfort. The daily calendar on my desk offers an inspirational read for each day. Subtly placed throughout my home are small decorative plaques that add to the positive atmosphere I prefer. They say things like "Live, Love, Laugh," "This is My Happy Place," and "Happily Ever After." One of my favorites is a little one I picked up on a vacation that reminds me to *"Read Books, Drink Wine," and "Be Happy."* Even the music television station that I play at home to enhance a relaxing environment displays uplifting quotes every few minutes. To be honest, I never paid much attention to them until one day I noticed a friend of mine enjoying reading them out loud.

Now I make it a point to read and ponder a couple of them each day. Another friend of mine has a special bookmark he has had for years. On it is a poem reminding him to never quit. He says that this poem has helped him to press on during some of the most stressful times of his life. Social media can also be a wonderful place to read and share joy, inspiration, and positivity if you choose to use it this way. When you find a meme or a positive saying, consider sharing it on your social media platform. Not only will you uplift others, you will also re-read it yourself from time to time as you review your own posts. Consider joining groups or connecting with others who share uplifting material so that you see and read it often. Remember that you get to decide what types of words and phrases you encounter each day. I encourage you to choose wisely.

- <u>Treat yourself to some pampering of your choice.</u> This is a simple, yet effective self-care technique. Some examples could be a massage, a facial, a manicure, or a pedicure. Go ahead, pamper yourself. You deserve it!

Chapter Two

GRATITUDE, VISUALIZATION, AND CREATING MOMENTUM TOWARD YOUR DESIRES

Gratitude

Notice, Appreciate, Repeat. Make this a way of life, and reap the benefits of habitually feeling good. Beauty is all around us. Kindness and love are all around us. All we have to do is take the time to *notice*. So many beautiful things in our world can be overlooked if we don't purposefully give our attention to them. Notice things throughout your day such as squirrels chasing each other, birds flying in formation, a beautiful flower, a person demonstrating kindness to another, or the friendly innocence of a toddler when your eyes meet. By doing this, you will have a more joyful experience than someone who rushes from task to task, missing the beauty that is offered all around. You will also cause neurons to connect in the brain which will increase the likelihood of you noticing objects of beauty more frequently. Speak and think often about what you appreciate, and watch them expand. Can you name at least five things right now for which you are grateful? They can be anything at all and be as big or as simple as you like. Your family? Your friends? The sound of the rain on the roof last night? Shelter? Health? The weather yesterday or the forecast for today? The things you appreciate can be spoken about, written about, focused upon, or all of the above. This is a great tool for uplifting your mood as well as helping you notice and experience even more things to appreciate throughout your day.

In my workbook entitled *Fill Your Cup Daily Journal*, I provide morning and evening sentence starters designed to improve daily life experiences through the purposeful focusing of one's thoughts. One of the sentence starters begins with the words "*I love.*" This simple prompt is intentionally designed to raise one's level of appreciation and mood in general, which is why I refer to it as "The Ultimate Focus Statement." These words are fun to list and think about at any time of day. Below is an excerpt from my workbook explaining how this sentence starter can be used.

THE ULTIMATE FOCUS STATEMENT
I LOVE...

What do you LOVE? What makes your heart sing? What brings you joy? Comfort? Enthusiasm? It may be the simplest things or things more extravagant. Snuggling up with a good book by a crackling fire on a cold winter's night? The ebb and flow of the ocean? The endless and ever-changing shapes, colors, and glorious displays of beauty in the vast sky? The sound of the rain? A baby's belly laugh? Candlelight and the peaceful serenity of a quiet evening? Or the rush of a good run, sail, or drive in or on your favorite vehicle? It could be things you love to do or things you love to see, hear, touch, smell, or taste. Anything that makes you feel good when you think about it is perfect for this list. Go on, start YOUR list. Write freely... What do YOU love? Appreciate? What brings you joy? Feel your spirits rise as you write down and focus on these things.

Add to the list whenever you want. Read it often, and make a point to NOTICE and appreciate the things in your world that align with this list. Then watch as the more you notice and appreciate them, the more they will tend to show up. It's amazing how this works!

One thing that I love to do is bask in the beauty of nature, so I make a point to do so each day. I find that the more I bask in nature's astounding beauty, the more beauty she shows to me. The sky changes by the minute sometimes, as if it's playfully saying,

"Do you like this view? Wait... Now how about this one? OK then, how do you like this one? And now? How do ya like me now?" These are my inner thoughts often as I watch the ever-changing morning or evening sky as if its sole purpose is to entertain and delight me.

I recently found some old lists I had written of things I love, and it's interesting how I really haven't changed much at the core. Below are some of my "I love's." Have fun listing yours! ☺

I love...

- *I love to look at the trees swaying in the wind*
- *I love peace and serenity*
- *I love peaceful music and the smell of sensual candles*
- *I love watching Little House on the Prairie with my kids*
- *I love a warm fire in the fireplace*
- *I love slippers, books, and journals*
- *I love taking pictures of beautiful nature and of my precious children*
- *I love TIME!!!!!!!!!*
- *I love having lots of time to do all of the many things I love to do such as read, write, exercise, meditate, bask, and prepare healthy and savory foods for myself and my family!*

I love...

- *The smell of a campfire*
- *Doing fun things with my kids*
- *Basking in a beautiful view*
- *Enjoying the sounds of the crickets and other beautiful sounds of the woods*

- *Sitting on the deck and reading, writing, or simply just being*
- *The feeling of being caught up on daily/weekly tasks, chores, and necessities*
- *Enjoying time with friends and family*

I could (and will) go on and on adding to this list. I encourage you to have fun with yours!

Visualization

When we want something, what we are ultimately seeking is the way we think we will feel once we have obtained our desire. Visualizing what you are yearning for as if it is already present can help you to obtain this wonderful feeling right now. The more you are able to experience the feelings of your fulfilled desires, the more you become a vibrational match to them; and consequently, the easier it is for them to manifest in your life. This is based on the law of attraction which simply put, states that like attracts like. We don't need to understand what that means in order to experience it in our lives. Here is an example. Have you ever had a day that just seemed to go consistently from bad to worse? Have you heard of the old saying, "When it rains, it pours."? Once negative momentum gets going, it attracts more negative experiences. Fortunately, the opposite is also true. If you can get the positive momentum going with your thoughts and feelings, this will in turn attract more positive experiences and people to you. I like to describe it as, "The better it gets, the better it gets." If you haven't noticed, what we focus on tends to increase in our experience, and there are so many examples that demonstrate this. To share just one, say you want a particular thing, and you begin researching it and thinking about it often. You will soon notice that you see it more and more while you are out and about. Where we focus our attention is very important because it affects our future experiences. For this reason, I like to use visualization as a tool to increase the momentum of positive thoughts, feelings, and experiences throughout my day.

It feels good to imagine myself feeling peace and appreciation for various blessings in my life as I move through the events of my day. For example, I like to envision positive interactions with others, full of kindness, compassion, playfulness, and laughter; I like to envision a productive day with the opportunity to help and inspire others. I try to make an effort to take a minute here and there to breathe in, breathe out, and picture what I want for the next portion of my day. For example, I might visualize a safe, peaceful, smooth ride to work followed by a happy, inspired, and productive morning with my coworkers. I imagine the feeling of fulfillment I get from helping others as I go through my workday. Later I might envision a relaxing commute home followed by a loving, productive, and joyful evening with my family. Focusing my thoughts in ways that make me feel good has been tremendously effective in positively shaping my daily experiences.

In the preceding paragraphs, I have described visualizing what you wish to experience throughout your day. Next, I will share some other ways to use visualization. One popular technique is to create a vision board. This is basically a collage filled with things that make you feel good and inspired when you look at them. For example, my vision board has pictures of beautiful homes and vacation destinations that make me feel wealthy and blessed. I had fun cutting them out of magazines, and I enjoy seeing them every day. I have a picture of my kids on it as well because seeing them always makes me smile and feel love. I also have inspiring words and phrases on my board such as "Health," "Fun," and "Life is Good." I even have an index card I wrote years ago describing the perfect job that I desired. I used to carry it around and read it often. Now on my board next to that card is my current business card as a reminder that the job I desired and described so long ago is the exact job I have and love today. This is a wonderful testimony demonstrating that focusing our thoughts really can impact our experiences. A vision board should be customized for the person who creates it, as we each have our own unique desires. The main goal is to fill it with things that make you feel good when you look at them.

I encourage you to take photographs or collect pictures that are visually appealing to you, whether they have manifested into your life yet or not. Look at them often, and feel the joy that they bring. You can use Instagram, Pinterest, a photo gallery, or any other platform you choose to help yourself focus on things you like and visualize what you want.

Another tool for visualization is writing. Describe what you want to experience as well as how you will feel when it happens. As you describe your desires, include as much or as little detail as you like, whatever feels good to you. You want any form of visualization to be a pleasurable experience in and of itself, not only for the benefit of feeling good now but also for the momentum of positive attraction that is added when one is feeling desired emotions. Remember, *"The better it gets, the better it gets."* It may sound strange at first, but the more you practice finding ways of feeling good, the more feeling good will become a natural and frequent state of being. Writing about our desires is a wonderful way to begin and sustain this process.

If writing is not your thing, no worries. Perhaps drawing is more your style. If this is the case, then by all means, go ahead and draw or sketch out pictures of whatever it is that you want. For example, grab a piece of paper and sketch or map out that dream home, and imagine how satisfying it feels to live there. I used to draw charts illustrating my academic journey toward earning my master's degrees. Seeing the coursework mapped out on paper helped me to see the progress I had made as well as what I had yet to complete in order to achieve my goals. If you can picture it in your mind and it feels good to do so, visualize whatever it is that you want and enjoy the process.

One way to jump-start the momentum toward a desire is something I like to call "*leaning into it.*" This is a method that I have found to be particularly effective. Sometimes we have a vision or a desire, but we don't currently know exactly *how* it will happen. That is perfectly okay. We don't have to have all of the details worked out in order to take a faithful step towards what we want, thus *leaning into it.* When I set off to get my master's in school counseling, I had *no idea* how I was going to afford it, much less how I would juggle it with my already busy schedule. Yet still, I wanted to take a step in the direction of my goal, so I borrowed enough money from my mom to pay for one class in order to start the process. I literally *leaned into it* and began feeling the experience of being a grad student. You don't have to know how you will afford a new vehicle or house to get out and test drive some cars or walk through some model homes. Doing these things can add a whole new dimension to visualizing and can assist you in experiencing the feeling of having achieved a desire. Doing this purely for fun, without the pressure of a specific time frame or detailed plan, is a great way to begin leaning toward a goal. It's also a fantastic way to enjoy the powerful visualization experience.

For example, something I have enjoyed many times with my kids is visiting model homes for sale, not because we were in the market for buying one at the time, but simply because it felt so good to do so. I always love the way they are decorated, and I get so much pleasure out of walking through them, imagining what it would feel like to live somewhere so beautiful. The kids enjoyed it as well as they happily picked out their rooms, so for a while, we did this quite often. In addition, for years I would drive to affluent neighborhoods to do my morning runs. I loved looking at the various mansions, and jogging through these communities helped me to envision what it would be like to live there. Eventually, I began making a special stop on the way home from these runs. I had come to a point in my life where I found myself dreaming often of purchasing our next home, and I happened to know where a new neighborhood would be built in the near future. It was nothing but a cornfield next to the woods at the time, but I used to drive my car up the tractor path next to the woods until I got halfway up the tree line. There I would turn off my car, get out, crouch down, and gaze into the woods, all the while imagining my home located right there. I pretended I was looking at my own backyard view, and it felt good to do so. I am not sure of the time frame, but months to a year later, we were able to sell our then-current home and buy the exact lot I had visited and visualized from so many times. The view that I had gazed upon all of those mornings after my runs is now the view behind my home that I get to enjoy every day.

Another demonstration of creating momentum towards something by leaning into it is the story of how we got our first dog. Prior to having a pet, my children and I used to visit the SPCA on Saturdays sometimes just for the fun of visiting and petting the dogs. Their dad was dead set against getting a pet, but we still enjoyed going and spending time with the animals. Eventually, we found one particular dog who captured our hearts. I decided to put a deposit on him so that they would hold him overnight for us, *just in case*. The idea was initially met with predictable resistance, but eventually, after many talks with the kids, little girl tears, backing off in quiet defeat, and then subtly sliding notes and pictures of the dog under our bedroom door the next morning, Dad finally softened his stance on the subject. Needless to say, that day we came home with our new dog Lucky.

One last and profound example of *leaning into it* that I will share is regarding the finishing of my basement. Years ago, while walking through my messy, unfinished basement with my then-boyfriend, he made the mistake of uttering five powerful words that drastically influenced the events of the next two years of our lives. Those words were, "I could finish your basement." *Wait, what?* I had no plan or budget for such a project, but his words prompted me to immediately say (before he changed his mind), "OK then, let's get some supplies and get started!"

With new energy turned toward this area of my home, I was inspired to go through some boxes and items that I had been putting off for years. After all, if we were going to take a step toward finishing the basement, I had better get rid of some unneeded things that were in the way. It just so happened that I owned a rare classic musical instrument that was worth a good amount of money. It was an instrument I loved and cherished but no longer needed or used. I listed it for sale and ended up selling it to a musician who appreciated its value and would cherish it as much as I had. This was very important to me because this instrument had a lot of history with my family and therefore much sentimental value. The exchange felt good, and the money it brought in paid for the initial materials to begin our project.

Unfortunately, I had misunderstood those initial words, "I could finish your basement." As it turned out, what he *actually* meant was, "*WE* could finish your basement," but so be it. I was dedicated to following this through and willing to roll up my sleeves and learn to do whatever needed to be done. It was a laborious two-year process as we worked through much sweat and sometimes tears (mine of course).

All the while though, I continually visualized the end result in my mind. I placed a vase filled with a beautiful palm branch on the dusty landing because it helped me to picture how peaceful it would look when it was finished. I spent many hours looking at the messy construction site while envisioning what I wanted it to become. I even put tape on the floor at one point to visualize where furniture would be placed.

I am not recommending this, but at the time I did not have a planned budget put aside for this incredible project. If I had known in the beginning just how huge this undertaking would be, I would have been too overwhelmed to even think it could be possible. As it happened though, I figured it out one load of supplies at a time over a two-year time span. We put in endless hours of grueling labor, but in hindsight, it was worth it. I was grateful that I had the blessing of a construction mastermind who was willing to head up the project without expecting monetary compensation. Little by little it progressed, and eventually, we finished it.

When the fun part of decorating finally began, things seemed to fall into place effortlessly. For example, a dear friend of mine was getting rid of some beautiful artwork that she no longer needed, and it just so happened that these pieces complimented my color scheme and were perfect for my walls.

This miraculous basement transformation would have never happened if it weren't for the inspiration at the very beginning when I heard those five little words, "I could finish your basement." I then promptly *leaned into it* without overthinking, thus putting the project into motion. Even though we may not know *how* something will be made possible, sometimes just believing enough to take one small step at a time towards a goal is enough.

Chapter Three

WHAT ARE YOU "INPUTTING"

One of the biggest influences on our inner thoughts, beliefs, and attitudes is what we "input" into our ears and eyes on a habitual basis. What do you listen to? What do you read? What do you watch? In what conversations do you choose to participate? These choices affect how you think, how you feel, and in turn, what you experience. Ultimately, you have the freedom to put into your own mind whatever you choose. However, I encourage you to make these decisions consciously and thoughtfully, for they can have a significant impact on your habitual feelings and experiences. In the words that follow, I will share some ways that I like to control what I feed my mind.

The first is regarding the news which I choose to avoid most of the time. I realize that I am likely in the minority regarding this choice, and I am okay with that. My thought is that if it's important or major enough that I should know about it, either someone will tell me, I will hear others discussing it, and/or I will see it on social media. The proportion of reported bad news vs. good news is simply not an accurate reflection of real life. What the news media portrays compared to what I witness in my daily experiences are, thank goodness, vastly different. I see much more kindness and compassion among people than the broadcasts would lead one to believe. The negative content of daily news stories is not what I choose to feed my brain on a regular basis. Instead, I prefer to make my own headlines, whether via thought, spoken word, or shared on social media. "New Rescue Dog Makes it all Day With No Housetraining Accidents," "Great Talk With a Parent Today," "Son Makes Dean's List," "Daughter Wins Music Contest," "Important Person in my Life Shares Their Appreciation of Me," "Pulled off a Great Dinner for the Family," "Early Spring Brings Beautiful Weather to Enjoy." These are the things I choose to focus on, and I am happier because of it.

Another way that I control what I put into my mind is my choice of what I listen to when I drive. I find that travel time is a great opportunity for conscious "inputting," and there is so much from which to choose. Perhaps you enjoy listening to music that makes you feel good. As someone with a musical background, I have several different styles of music that I enjoy, and which one I choose to listen to at any given time, depends on my mood. I have made many a road trip much more fun by listening to old-school funk or other upbeat music. On the contrary, when I taught piano lessons full time and was constantly immersed in music, I actually preferred silence or talk radio in the car for a change of pace. Perhaps there is a book you would like to read for pleasure, education, or inspiration. Commuting time can be a perfect opportunity to listen to audiobooks. For years I have listened to inspirational speakers while driving, turning necessary commutes into uplifting experiences. Although I still enjoy inspirational audio, lately I have been listening to comedians while driving, enjoying the lightheartedness of humor and the feeling of a good laugh. Commuting provides us with a wonderful opportunity for conscious inputting. Choose thoughtfully, and turn this tedious time into a positive and meaningful part of your day.

Another common form of feeding the mind is through reading. What do you like to read? Does it lift you up or bring you joy? Reading provides opportunities for self-care in many ways. Looking back to a time in my life when I felt as if I needed emotional healing, books provided me with many tools to assist with that journey. Whether it was self-help, personal development, spiritual support, daily devotions and inspirations, or relationship advice, books were always there to support me with knowledge, input, and comfort. Even after healing took place, books continued to accompany me in my life for personal development, enjoyment, and education. I believe in life-long learning; there is always room to grow, improve, and increase our knowledge on subjects of interest. Since there are nonfiction books written on pretty much every subject imaginable, the sky is the limit.

Fiction books on the other hand, also provide wonderful opportunities for self-care, as they are intended primarily for entertainment and enjoyment. A good book can pique my interest, stimulate my mind, and temporarily transport me into another world as I get lost in the stories of the characters. Making a point to set aside time to read (and then following through on it) is a direct act of self-care. For years I claimed to love reading, yet rarely engaged in it. Why? Because I was not making myself a priority. There is always something else to do or tend to, so in order to incorporate reading back into my life, I had to purposely set this intention and follow through on it. Have I succeeded 100%? Of course not, but it is something that I value and therefore will continue prioritizing. One final note about reading: It is a great way to constructively and/or positively pass time when I would otherwise be doing nothing more than waiting for something to occur. Whether it be waiting in the car for someone, standing in a long line, or sitting in a room awaiting an appointment, reading provides a great opportunity to enjoy something I love, thus making the wait time more constructive.

Another avenue of mind "inputting" that most of us engage in is watching television, which leads to the question of what to watch. There is such a wide array of choices available to us, and we all have our own personal preferences. This is a good thing because variety is what makes the world go 'round. I think what matters most when choosing our television entertainment is how we feel when we are watching. Does what you watch make you laugh, make you feel warm and fuzzy, grasp your attention, or intrigue your mind with new knowledge? If so, wonderful! Maybe you crave something silly or mindless just to give your brain a break after a long day. Also wonderful. What I encourage is having an awareness of how what you watch makes you feel so that you can choose purposefully.

Do you ever find that what you chose to watch affects your thoughts even after you have finished watching? If so, pay careful attention because our brains are sponges. Once, while navigating a new relationship, I was invited to watch a gory horror show with my partner. Although I knew that this was not something I would normally choose to watch, in the name of being open-minded, I agreed. I remember feeling incredibly disturbed by what I saw on the screen, images I absolutely did not want in my mind. I instantly felt the discord physically as well as emotionally and actually had to leave the room and step outside in an attempt to regain my emotional balance. Admittedly, I may be more sensitive than many, but that experience provides an example of listening to the guidance of your emotions when deciding what is right for you. While this man thoroughly enjoyed watching this type of show, it was clearly not something I wanted to include in my experience. Regardless of what you choose to watch for your entertainment purposes, be mindful of how it makes you feel both during and post-viewing time. If you enjoy these thoughts and feelings, then it is likely a good choice for you.

Lastly, in discussing what you allow to be inputted into your sensory system, let's visit the subject of conversations, which are ever-present in the lives of most people. Conversations are powerful. They involve thoughts, words, and communion with others. We are, after all, social beings by nature. Have you heard it said that those who complain attract much to complain about? I am a believer in this statement, and I see it evidenced often in the lives of others whom I observe. Have you ever spent time with someone who habitually complains and speaks negatively? I do not recommend it, as it can be extremely draining. Instead, I recommend surrounding yourself with people who tend to be more positive and immersing yourself in uplifting conversations. Making this simple choice regarding the company you keep and the conversations you participate in can be life-giving and life-changing. I know it has been for me. Does that mean I never complain? Certainly not; I am far from perfect. I do try though, to notice the silver lining in any given situation, and consequently, I have found many throughout my life.

I also try to notice and point out the good in people as often as possible. Even when someone has created an undesirable outcome, this doesn't necessarily mean that their intention was malice. A couple of wise women I know often say, "Assume positive intent." After all, we are all doing the best we can with what we have at the time, and sometimes grace can be a better choice than judgment. Each of us is a work in progress, present company included. If we can see the *glass-half-full* side of a person or a situation, I believe it is important to do so and noteworthy enough to share with others.

I am happy to say that most of my closest people are optimists like I am, at least in most situations. We are like-minded and enjoy sharing blessings and encouraging each other. Despite being an introvert at heart and needing much time for solitude, great conversations happen to be one of my favorite things in the world. Sharing ideas, inspirations, dreams, and encouragement can be life-giving. My family on my dad's side has an outdoor gazebo with a large table and many chairs. Oh, the stories that table could tell! I can't begin to count the many conversations with family and friends that have been shared around that table. From quick-witted and open-minded discussions about topics with varying opinions, to laughter over stories told and retold about crazy memories over the years, to ideas and inspirations shared and encouraged, to confidences revealed with support and encouragement provided, that table has been the centerpiece of many of my favorite conversations and greatest memories. It is my hope that many families and/or friends have a similar gathering place (or consider creating one), because communion with loved ones is priceless.

Just as what we feed our body affects the level of physical health that we experience, it is no different with our minds. What we listen to, read, watch, and converse about are forming and shaping our thoughts and attitudes on a continual basis, thus, naturally affecting our experiences. What we allow to be *inputted* into our minds is a perpetual choice that we get to make every day. Who and what we surround ourselves with naturally influences who we are, as well as whom we become as we evolve on our life's journey. We truly do reap what we sow, so as you plant the seeds in your mind via your daily choices of input, may your resulting harvest of life's rewards bring much joy and satisfaction.

Chapter Four

CREATING YOUR OPTIMAL ENVIRONMENT

How do you Decorate Your Space?

Physical space contains energy. This is evidenced in the Chinese study of Feng shui, an ancient and widely used practice that focuses on the flow of energy in physical space in order to design living or working areas for maximum harmony, balance, and positive benefit. Spatial energy has the ability to instill feelings, emotions, and states of being ranging from peacefulness to excitement, to over-stimulation. Imagine that feeling of reverence when entering a place of worship, or the feeling of excitement and anticipation when entering a desired place of entertainment such as an amusement park, sports event, or concert. What you prefer is unique to you and may change as you progress through various stages of your life. How do you want to feel in your home as well as your workspace, and what can you do to your environments to evoke these desired feelings? Acknowledge what aesthetics bring you a sense of peace, calmness, and/or joy, and aspire to surround yourself with them.

I am particularly sensitive to the energy of my physical environment. Therefore, setting up my physical space is of significant importance. As aforementioned, I used to walk through model homes for the pure pleasure of how it felt to be in them, and I am confident that the decorators were experts at purposely instilling such positive feelings in potential buyers. I took ideas from them and vowed to eventually transform my own space to make me feel the way I felt in these homes. I am happy to say that I have been successful in this area, and I will share various ways in which I have done so. My home is my safe haven. Its purpose is to emanate warmth and comfort for me as well as my loved ones. I like my home to have a feeling of calmness, and I am adamant about maintaining this environment in my living space.

I am also conscious of my workspace. When I was a teacher I decorated my walls with positive affirmations and uplifting statements and often played calming music in the background. While my home was *my* safe haven, for all I know, this classroom may have been the safe haven for any number of my students, and it was my job to create that for them. The environment I provided, coupled with other things I did to instill in my students that they were respected and cared for, paid off a thousandfold. Many students displayed a completely different (much calmer and more respectful) personality in my room than in other classrooms. Currently, as a school counselor, I often have students tell me that they enjoy being in my office because it makes them feel safe and calm. They often express that they love my water fountain, office tree, quiet music, and various tactile items designed for different types of students and occasions. This always feels good to hear because that was my intention when I designed this space.

The Visual Aesthetics of Your Environment

As you think about creating your ultimate environment, think about what you like to see around you. Do you prefer lots of knick-knacks, or do you like more space and less clutter? What feelings well up within you as you imagine each one? Do you like to decorate with a theme or more generally? What sort of items do you like to display in your surroundings? Favorite artwork? Meaningful or beautiful home accessories on tables, shelves, or walls, or do you prefer your shelves stocked with books? Perhaps it depends on the room. In general, I enjoy surrounding myself with things that symbolize calmness or meditation. In my bedroom, I have a small bookshelf corner that houses my favorite books and thus brings me comfort. In my main living areas, I like to include aesthetically pleasing items such as wall decor, vases, and candles. I also incorporate objects that have special meaning such as beautiful stones and art from my various travels, and a meditation bowl I purchased from a woman in Mexico.

Each one holds the energy of fond traveling memories and the people I have connected with along the way.

Color choices also play a factor in the development of your physical environment. The psychology of color is the study of the effects color can have on mood and emotions, and it has been considered widely in marketing and interior design. It incorporates the belief that colors can either stimulate or soothe the body and mind. Is there a particular color scheme that you like? It's perfectly normal if your preference changes as you grow and evolve. For example, I used to like cool colors such as blues and grays, yet now I lean towards earthy colors such as sage green, tans, and burgundies. I also enjoy having live greenery scattered about, as plants offer a healthy and grounding connection to nature. Which colors tend to bring you your desired state of being? If you are conscious of these preferences, it is fun to surround yourself with them when decorating your personal space.

Next, consider lighting. What do you prefer in various environments? Lighting can have a powerful effect on the mood or feeling of an area. Do you prefer it bright or dim? During the day I like the natural lighting of the outdoors, but as the day progresses and indoor light becomes favorable, I usually have my general living area lit with soft lighting which I find welcoming and relaxing. I am not a fan of fluorescent lighting, and therefore avoid going to department stores in the evening when at all possible. At work, several colleagues and I keep our fluorescent ceiling lights off and instead work to the natural outdoor lighting coupled with a few functionally placed lamps.

During the fall and winter, I find comfort in various forms of lighting, such as a flickering fireplace and candles. I particularly love the flameless automatic candles that I have placed around my family room. They are set to come on at a certain time when it's getting dark, and they go off automatically a set number of hours later. I love that they light up for me each day as evening approaches, reminding me of my brother who gifted them to me one Christmas. They look authentic and help set a relaxing tone each evening. Other automatic lights that make me happy are the battery-powered window candles that light up my home each evening in the colder months, and also the solar lights on my deck railings that light up every night and beckon me to step outside to enjoy the view.

Holiday lights bring joy to many, myself included. While some prefer a busy, colorful, and showy display of outdoor lights on their homes, I prefer a more subtle look of white lights and window candles, making it feel like a joyful and welcoming place. On the inside, I love the garland and white lights that decorate my fireplace mantle and stair railings. One year after thoroughly enjoying how the Christmas tree lights warmly illuminated a corner of the room, I felt a void in that area when the tree was taken down. To remedy this, I replaced it with a palm tree decorated with white lights. It's amazing how that subtly lit plant corner improved the overall atmosphere of the room, so much so, that I keep lights up year-round on both my family room palm as well as a floor plant in my living room. I love that these areas are never completely dark, but always softly illuminated with the romantic lighting of white lights. Take a moment to contemplate your own lighting preferences and take steps towards creating visual surroundings that feel good to you.

Another way to improve the feel of your environment is to reduce clutter. Clean out a closet or organize a space such as a drawer or a cupboard. This not only achieves a sense of accomplishment, it also helps to open up space so that the energy of the area can flow more naturally. Decluttering can be applied electronically as well. Unsubscribing to junk email and clearing out your inbox can feel absolutely wonderful. Whether online or in-person, a clear space is often associated with a clear mind, just as a cluttered and disorganized space often reflects and/or creates a mind with similar chaos. That being said, my daughter, who has always been a creator, pointed out another perspective. Sometimes when she completely gives in to her muse and is in the throes of creation, her outer environment may get neglected for a time, and that is okay. She has committed fully to the creative process, and that becomes her current priority. I see her point, have lived this truth as well, and see the value in looking at things from different perspectives. Life naturally ebbs and flows. There is no absolute right or wrong way. We are all on our own ever-changing paths with our own desires, opinions, and perspectives. Experiment, find what works for you, and enjoy your journey.

How Do You Want Your Environment to Sound?

In addition to visual surroundings, I also value the use of sounds when creating the tone and mood of my spaces. Imagine for a moment the sounds you might hear when you walk into a spa or a massage room. What type of music might be playing in the background? Perhaps there is a fountain of some sort with the sound of trickling water. These things are all purposefully implemented to infuse a sense of calmness and serenity in the clients. Now imagine the sounds you might hear before a big sports event, such as loud music, the sounds of an excited crowd, and the power and hype of a drumline, all intended to build excitement and anticipation for the impending event. Music in particular moves people's emotions in a profound way. Think of the tears that well up when someone sings a powerful song, or the emotions in various church congregations during inspirational musical performances. Music and sound have a direct link to our moods and emotions, so why not use this to our advantage when setting up our own environments?

What type of sounds do *you* like to hear as you spend time in your living and work spaces? Some people like complete silence, while others like to hear the television (or radio) in the background because they like hearing the sound of human voices. Some say it keeps them company. I, on the other hand, absolutely cringe at the sound of the TV in the background (with the exception of football) unless I have intentionally sat down to watch something. Instead, I like quiet, calming music to set the atmosphere, preferably without words so that the music can serve as a backdrop to a relaxing environment without interrupting my thoughts or productivity. (Of course, depending on the time of day and what I am doing, this music choice can change as I love and appreciate *many* different types of music.) When creating my general auditory background, another thing I enjoy is the soothing sound of trickling water. Because of this, I often place a fountain in my most used and loved areas. Give some thought to your own auditory preferences and surround yourself with them whenever you can.

What Else Would Bring Comfort and Well-being to Your Environment?

What else would make your most frequented areas feel welcoming and comforting to you? At work, pictures of my children keep me feeling connected to them and also occasionally serve as conversation starters. Some things that I love in my home are scented candles, comfy throw pillows, and warm, soft blankets. What are your preferences? Give it some thought and purposefully lean towards making your environment uniquely you. It's your space, after all, so it might as well make you feel wonderful when you enter it.

Chapter Five

YOUR DAILY ROUTINES

Daily routines can be a positive influence in our lives, especially if we design them to align with our life goals and values. For example, if physical fitness is a priority to you, it would make sense to incorporate a form of exercise into your regular routine. By following a routine of specific repeated actions, habits are created. Once something becomes a habit, it is much easier to stick with it. It becomes part of what you do on a regular basis and can become as automatic as brushing your teeth in the morning. On the other hand, have you ever noticed that after skipping a few days of doing something, it becomes that much harder to get back into it? Using exercise as an example, after missing a few days, it's as if not-exercising becomes the new norm. The saying that we are creatures of habit rings true, so whatever action(s) you choose to incorporate into your regular routine, remember that it is the repetition of these actions that forms the habit, which in turn makes it easier to continue to do them regularly with less effort. It is good self-care practice to consider your goals and values as you thoughtfully design your daily routines.

Undoubtedly there is as much variety in preferred routines as there is with people and their differing personalities and preferences. This is perfectly normal given the diversity of our world. In pondering the variety in people's schedules and routines, and appreciating that everyone gets to choose what serves them best, an example comes to mind regarding the vast difference in sleep routines between one of my brothers and myself. He usually gets up sometime in the afternoon and is up until the wee hours of the morning either working or creating, while I am deep in slumber. He then goes to bed pretty close to the time that I get up. In the evenings when I am winding down from my day, he is gearing up for his. Although our sleep schedules are polar opposites, one is no better than the other. His serves his lifestyle, and mine serves mine. Fortunately for our relationship, there is a window of time in the afternoons and earlier part of the evenings that allows us time to visit and socialize. At the same time, our differing sleep schedules provide a balance that allows us each some time for solitude, adding a nice yin and yang to our visits.

Morning Routine

How would you describe your perfect morning routine? If you are a night owl, perhaps you are one who enjoys sleeping in, replenishing your energy for a productive day and evening to follow. On the other hand, if you are a morning person like me, you tend to be more productive and energetic in the mornings. I value the importance of setting myself up for a positive and productive day by incorporating a flexible morning routine. I say flexible because each day has its own influences, and there are some days when my routine needs to be adjusted accordingly. Perhaps I was up way too late the night before for some reason, or a person or pet needed extra attention, support, or care. While my routine is important because it creates habits that I choose to incorporate into my life, it is also important to be able to adjust to daily influences as needed without self judgement. After all, it's my life, and I get to make and/or break the rules as I see fit. Even if it gets altered once in a while due to circumstances, having a thoughtfully chosen routine is helpful in meeting my personal goals, which in turn affects how I feel each day. Sticking with the example of exercising, since it has become habitual, it remains fairly easy to continue regularly, and because it is part of my daily morning routine, if I miss a day or two (because of necessary or chosen adjustments) five or six days a week is still a good track record for success.

If I did everything I would like to do for a morning routine it would probably take all morning long. For those who have this kind of time, wonderful!! For those of us who have a limited amount of time in the morning before obligations begin, we need to prioritize. Take a moment to ponder, what sets you up for a happy day? One suggestion I have that is not time-consuming is to wake up with gratitude. Think about something or some things in your life for which you are grateful. As you focus on them, feel the joy and appreciation that they bring. Perhaps it is the feel of your pillows, the warmth of your bed, and/or the shelter of your home. Maybe it is for your loved ones and/or your pets. Perhaps it is that you have a job to go to, or even that you don't, depending on your current stage in life. There are so many things from which to choose no matter how big or how small. As discussed previously, appreciation can enhance daily joy immensely; remember, just as complainers tend to attract much to complain about, people who focus on what they are grateful for tend to find themselves with even more to appreciate. Why not use this powerful knowledge to your advantage, and purposely wake up with gratitude. What a positive way to begin your day!

I know some who like to hop out of bed immediately in the mornings to start their day, and for them, this works perfectly. Although I have lived this way in the past, I am at a place in my life now where I like to lean into my day slowly. I don't prefer to hop right out of bed at the first sound of my alarm. Instead, I like to bask in the feeling of being awake and propped up with pillows while still appreciating the comfort of being all cuddled up under my covers. I enjoy this early morning quiet time so much that I set my alarm for thirty minutes before I need to get out of bed. This block of me-time is a self-care gift I indulge in almost every day. I enjoy it so much that it is easily worth the price of going to bed earlier than most in order to be able to fit this time into my routine. While basking in feelings of gratitude, these thirty minutes allow me time to meditate if I choose, as well as time to read, check the weather, etc. While I realize that this wake-up routine may not be for everyone, perhaps there are some who would enjoy it or something similar.

After my morning *me-time*, I move on to the next phase of my morning routine which takes place in the kitchen. Here I let out and feed the dogs, prepare my coffee and green juice for work, prep the next day's coffee to automatically brew, and load up my car. Although these are all things that need to be done, as aforementioned, I like puttering around in my kitchen. Therefore, this time is not only productive, it is also enjoyable.

Next comes my morning workout. As discussed earlier, any type of exercise should be tailored to what is best for each individual. I know what works for me has changed over the years, but I still make it a priority for supporting a healthy lifestyle. I know some who prefer to exercise after work or in the evenings to relieve the stress of the day, and that certainly does make sense. We are all unique, and everyone gets to decide what works best for them based on their own schedules. I choose to do my exercise in the morning, for I am self-aware enough to know that if I let too much time pass between getting up and exercising, I will inevitably get caught up in the tasks and momentum of the day. In turn, the discipline and inspiration to exercise will dissipate. For this reason, I make it part of my morning routine. Exercising in the mornings also helps me to feel proud of myself for being successful at starting my day doing something that I deem so valuable to my physical and mental well-being. I almost always feel better about myself and my morning if I have exercised.

I have some dear friends who have a morning routine that I admire. I imagine that it probably shifts and adjusts like everything else, but I have been inspired by them often enough that I will share my account of their morning routine. For them, like many, it begins with coffee. He typically brings her a cup (I know, how sweet!), and then he goes downstairs for some alone time to meditate. He has shared what a positive impact it has on him when he incorporates this ritual into his morning. In the meantime, his wife gets her own alone time to sip her coffee in bed and read. She, like me, also likes to ease into her day.

Later, they join each other for a workout of yoga and/or something similar. They both have a lot going on in their day-to-day business, so the fact that they make it a point to take time to prioritize balance is inspiring, to say the least. They are both highly successful people, so clearly they are doing something right. Fortunately, we can all learn from and receive inspiration from each other by seeing what successful routines others are incorporating into their lives.

Another suggested idea to include in a morning (or evening) routine is some time outside, for the outdoors can do wonders for the soul. Happily, I observe several people in my neighborhood dedicated to their outside morning routines, whether it be walking their dog(s), taking a jog, or walking with neighbors and friends. My outdoor morning run used to provide this for me, and I enjoyed it immensely for years. However, as time has passed my routine has shifted. I now do my daily exercise on my treadmill, and I get my A.M. dose of nature on my deck- first thing in the morning when I let my dogs out. It is quiet and peaceful then, soothing to my state of mind. Occasionally I will see a neighbor also soaking up the serenity of the morning, and we wave in silence, each respecting the other's tranquil moment. Later, at the beginning of my workday, I have outside duty supervising the students before they come into the school. Fortunately, the sky is often breathtaking at that hour, so I get a bit of a nature fix then as well. However brief it may be, if you are able to fit nature into your morning routine in any capacity that works for you, I strongly recommend it.

There are many personal development authors and coaches who promote morning journaling. Whether it be to record and contemplate one's dreams, journal about experiences, thoughts, or emotions, focus on blessings, or set a purpose and intention for the day, morning journaling is encouraged.

I wrote my first book *Fill Your Cup* as a workbook for journaling. It has morning and evening sentence starters intended to help people purposefully focus their thoughts in a way that improves their general mood and feelings. I originally created it purely for my own journaling purposes. However, I loved the positive effect it had on my mindset and daily experiences so much that I decided it was worth sharing, in the hopes that it could benefit others as well. Now republished as *Fill Your Cup Daily Journal,* it is an excellent way to pre-pave your day, live your life with purpose, and experience more gratitude and joy in your daily life.

Evening Routine

How do you like to enjoy your evenings? For those who are night owls, perhaps you work at night or enjoy doing productive tasks at home. I know several people who fit into this category, and there was a time in my life when I did as well. Perhaps you find purpose by serving on a committee, taking a class, or taking part in other evening events. I know many who enjoy these things on a regular basis and get much fulfillment out of doing so.

I tend to prefer a quiet and calming evening routine. Just as I like to ease into my day through the use of my morning routine, I also like to ease into the night by winding down in the evenings. As stated earlier, I cannot jump from the tasks and events of the day right into slumber. That does not work for me. Instead, I have a number of things I like to do that support my winding-down process. They make my evenings enjoyable and the sleep that follows peaceful and sound.

With my day beginning as early as it does (having been up and productive for about three hours before my workday begins), by the time the late afternoon and early evening approach, I am in need of *filling my cup.* After expending physical and emotional energy throughout the day, this is the time I need to refuel, and I take great pleasure in the various ways I do so. One of my favorite things to do after a long day is cuddling up on the couch with a bowl of popcorn to watch something on TV. Perhaps this could be referred to as a guilty pleasure, except I don't feel guilty about it at all. I feel as if I've earned it, and I enjoy the relaxation it provides. A similar yet equally relaxing suggestion is to curl up by a fire or someplace cozy with an inspiring, comforting, or just plain good book. This is especially fun in the wintertime or on a rainy day.

Something that I learned from my father is the joy of basking in the beauty of nature. Although this is wonderful to do at any time during the day, it is something that we especially enjoy doing while winding down in the evenings. I have most certainly inherited my dad's love and appreciation for a beautiful view, and for this I am grateful. Countless times we have sat at his place overlooking the various views of nature, enjoying our time appreciating it together. Many other evenings we have done the same thing over the phone, each sharing the beauty we see with the other. I also cherish nature's beauty by myself quite frequently (or with anyone caring to join me) as it is one of my favorite things to do. How I love sitting out on my deck in the evenings appreciating the beautiful view along with its melodious accompaniment of wind chimes and various sounds of the woods! I know that I will always connect this love of mine to my father, whose passion for life has overflowed into my own.

I feel it is worth recognizing here that the vast beauty of nature is available in some locations more than others. Therefore, focusing on beauty can be adjusted to what is available in your current environment. For example, when I lived in the city, a rooftop was a popular place for admiring the evening stars. Sometimes from the pavement of my front "yard," looking up at the sky was the most natural scene available. Perhaps you see a bird, a tree, or anything else representative of nature. These can all be things to enjoy and appreciate. It doesn't even always have to be nature per se. A city skyline, a beautiful building, a piece of art, or a beautifully decorated room, can all be worthy of being the subject of one's appreciation. Give your attention to any beauty available to you, notice how it makes you feel, and consider adding a little basking to your evenings.

Something else that makes me happy in the evenings is knowing that I have reached out via phone and talked with my parents either earlier in the day or at that moment. I love staying connected with them, and they always have something interesting to share. I enjoy, cherish, and appreciate every one of our conversations. I don't know how this is, but we never seem to run out of things to discuss. Although my preferred method of keeping in touch with other family and friends (when an in-person visit has not been scheduled) is via text, email, and/or social media, when it comes to my parents, phone chats are by far the best. Is there someone in your life with whom you enjoy chatting? Is there someone who would love it if you reached out to them for a conversation? Perhaps you have the opportunity to make someone's day, or your own for that matter, via a human connection. Whether it be with someone you live with or someone you reach out to, if you have the opportunity in your life to enjoy a positive connection with someone, consider yourself blessed. I know I do.

What constitutes an enjoyable evening for you? Whatever it is, I encourage you to be self-aware enough to identify it and disciplined enough to experience it as often as possible.

Other Routines, Priorities, and Stolen Moments

I believe it is good to listen to our moods and inspirations as we carry out our regular routines. By moods, I mean being sensitive to how you are feeling and recognizing when you need to fill your cup so that you don't run dry. By inspirations, I mean recognizing when you feel most inspired to do x, y, or z, and following that inner guidance. Morning people know that they tend to be more energetic and productive in the mornings while night owls feel the same about their evenings. If they set their daily schedule accordingly, life becomes naturally easier for them. For example, when I was self-employed I would do my scheduling, phone calls, and bookkeeping in the mornings because that is when my self-starting skills are at their peak. I generally don't feel as motivated in the afternoons, but I learned that if my time is scheduled to a commitment of some sort, this keeps me focused and productive during these hours. This is why teaching my students in the afternoons and early evenings worked perfectly for me. While I might not have been inspired to do desk work in the afternoons, I was fully engaged with my students when I taught them, thus making the best use of this time of day. Similarly, when I was an undergraduate student, I noticed that I tended to be least motivated and productive between the afternoon hours of three and six. For this reason, I signed up to work my part-time job during these hours. Because I was at work, I was forced to be productive, and in turn, I was able to spend my afternoons in a useful manner.

In addition to regular routines and schedules, I also believe that it's important to pay attention to how we are feeling in the moment on any given day. If at some point our energy level is low, could it simply mean that we need some time to slow down and recharge? I believe that our feelings and energy levels communicate to us regularly, letting us know when we need to create some balance and engage in self-care. An example of how I attempt to honor my current mood and energy level is the way I spend many Friday evenings and Saturday mornings. By Friday afternoon, the week has been long, and after a busy work week, a number of domestic tasks have piled up and are in need of time and attention. Perhaps the dishwasher needs to be emptied, things need tidying, or any number of other chores need tending. Although I do have some friends who like to knock out domestic tasks in the evenings, for me, it's unlikely to happen. By Friday evening my motivation level for production is zero, and my self-care cup needs filling. At this time I crave nothing more than to put on comfy clothes and relax, which is exactly what I do if I don't have a commitment that obligates me otherwise. Interestingly enough, I have not always been this way. Perhaps it's an age and stage thing, for I remember when I was in college, Friday evenings were a time to go out, hang with friends, and release the stress of the week. So as with everything else in life, to each his own. However, for me right now, there will be nothing productive happening on a typical Friday night. In the name of honoring the whole point of this book though, let me rephrase that statement. *Chores* are not likely to happen on a Friday night, because when my cup needs refilling, the most *productive* thing I can do is to recharge by honoring and tending to some self-care.

As you reflect on your own routines, I encourage you to think about what makes you feel good and incorporate these things regularly to the best of your ability. If there is something simple that you love to do such as read, write, draw, paint, dance, play an instrument, take a walk, or any hobby you love or have always wanted to do, I recommend making it a point to include it in your life. As they say, we only live once. If it brings you joy, by all means, do it. Don't leave it until last on your list only to get pushed aside after the hustle and bustle of a busy day. As I mentioned earlier, there were years when I never took the time out to read a good book, even though it's something I really love to do. It seemed as if there was never enough time to fit it in before the day's end. Now I make a point of setting aside time to read every day, even if it's just for a short amount of time. Think of something you love to do. Are you making it a priority when planning your time? If not, doing so would be a wonderful way to engage in self-care. Other people and obligations are important, yes, but you are equally important. The people who truly love you will want you to be the happiest and healthiest person you can be, and regular self-care is a huge step in that direction.

I will now share a few of my own self-care practices that I like to refer to as *stolen moments*. I find that if you have a busy schedule, you sometimes have to sneak in moments of self-care whenever you can. The following is one of my morning routine *stolen moments* and how it came to be. When my children were in middle school, they attended the school where I work. They were both in the band, and daily band rehearsals began about 35-40 minutes before the start of my workday. Since I did not desire to go to work that early every day, I was left with the choice of what to do with this interim time. It was certainly not long enough to drive home, and if I were to drive to a local establishment for coffee, most of my time would be taken up by the drive. However, there is a beautiful golf course only three minutes from the school, where the view is heavenly, and the sunrises are breathtaking. After dropping the kids off for band practice, I developed a habit of driving over to the golf course, parking my car, and enjoying half an hour of downtime. As it turns out, this ended up being one of the highlights of my day; it gave me precious alone time to sip my coffee, gather my thoughts, read, meditate, or do whatever I wanted to do. Anyone who has a busy life of family obligations will surely be able to relate to what a blessing it is to have thirty minutes to yourself. One of my very favorite things to do during my golf course time is to indulge myself in a good book. As aforementioned, reading is one thing that I love but couldn't previously seem to fit into my day. Now it had a set block of time worked right into my daily schedule. I learned quickly that I actually prefer not driving directly to work and immediately beginning the tasks of my day. My time at the golf course became the perfect pause prior to work; it left me feeling refreshed and ready to take on the day with a healthy mindset. As it always does though, time passed in the blink of an eye and soon my kids were no longer in middle school. In turn, I no longer needed to go in early as I had been doing for years. Was I willing to give up this sacred time I had so grown to love? Absolutely not; it was too important to me. I continued to leave extra early for work in order to park at that golf course for anywhere from five to thirty minutes every day just to sip my coffee, read a book, and enjoy some self-care time at the beginning of my day.

Let's now fast forward to a time later in the day. Imagine this: You get home from a long day of work, walk in the door, and are immediately greeted with requests.

Requests of your time, your attention, and a slew of other things. Perhaps it's a spouse wanting to tell you about his or her day before you even have a chance to catch your breath. Perhaps it's the dog who needs to go out, or worse, doesn't because he already "took care of that." Or perhaps you have children with their own sets of needs. It might sound something like this: *Mom, mom...mom. I'm hungry. Can you help me with _____?* And the list goes on. Sound familiar? Oh, and if you have young children, you are well aware that they pretty much demand one hundred percent of your time and attention during every waking moment (and sometimes the sleeping ones as well). I don't know about you, but for me, going immediately from the demands of work into the responsibilities of domestic life can be stressful, and a stressed-out parent or family member isn't a very fun person to be around. I find that if I can build in some sort of time to have a few minutes to myself before entering into the next phase of my day, this becomes a stolen moment that is very beneficial. Even just a brief chunk of time to recharge or top off my mental well-being tank can do wonders for my mindset, my attitude, and my patience level.

When my children were very young and spent their days at the daycare (located around the corner from our home), I was able to build in some recharging time prior to picking them up. If you've ever taken care of small children by yourself, you know how challenging it can be to fix a meal with them underfoot with their various needs. To combat this challenge, I would often stop home briefly before picking them up. This gave me the opportunity to drop off my things and do a few quick tasks such as rinse off my lunch dishes, open (or simply stack) the mail, and perhaps begin a little dinner prep, anything to make it so that I had more undivided attention to offer my children once they were home. This short stop home for Mom was a stolen moment of time that helped the rest of the day go smoother for everyone, and the daycare being so close by allowed me this luxury. Taking advantage of this stolen moment not only helped me by providing a few minutes of productive quietness between work and mothering, it also helped to prevent my small children from becoming upset when they couldn't have their mommy's full attention upon arriving home, which in turn would result in a tired and frustrated mom. Nobody wins in that situation. That quick stop at home before heading to the daycare really helped me transition from work to parenting. At the same time, it allowed my children to receive more of the undivided attention from their mommy that they so craved and deserved after not seeing her all day.

Although my children are older now, the demands of domestic life still prevail. Even the minutest task of opening and dealing with the mail can be difficult to complete on a busy weeknight. I have tried different methods of handling this, some proving to be more successful than others. For example, I have tried saving it for the weekend, but that usually ended up being a complete failure. The weekend would come, and I would dread dealing with what had now become a big pile of mail. Sometimes I just wouldn't get to it, and by the next weekend, the awaiting mail was even more overwhelming.

I have found that my most recent method of handling the mail has worked the best. It also provides me with a brief moment of quiet time to catch my breath prior to transitioning into my domestic life. When I arrive home from work each day I don't immediately pull into the garage and enter the house. Instead, I park next to my mailbox, pull out the mail, and open it right there in the car before anyone even knows I'm home. If you are a mom you know you will be bombarded the instant you walk in the door, so this is a way of stealing a moment for yourself prior to going in. If there are kids or dogs inside that need my attention, I know that opening mail anytime soon in their presence could prove to be a challenge. By opening it and sorting it in the car, I allow myself the uninterrupted time to do so without someone else feeling neglected. I am also able to drop any junk mail into the recycle bin and avoid bringing it into my home altogether. Even though this is a quick and simple little thing that I do, it is another one of the stolen moments that I find beneficial to the flow of my days and weeks. As you contemplate your own needs, challenges, and schedule, I hope that you will feel inspired to find opportunities to insert some of your own stolen moments: moments that could benefit the flow of your days and improve your self-care practice.

Chapter Six

IF IT'S A PRIORITY, SCHEDULE IT

Many years ago while spending a Saturday night hanging out and playing cards with a couple of good friends and neighbors, someone made the comment, "We always have so much fun when we all get together like this. How is it that we let so much time go by since the last time?" Everyone agreed, and we all said we absolutely need to do this more often. Then inevitably it happened again, time got away from us, and we ended up repeating the same conversation the next card night. Finally, we acknowledged the obvious. Because we are all so busy, if something is not scheduled on the calendar, it doesn't happen. We all agreed that we would like to get together like this once a month, so we began putting it on our calendars so that it would actually happen on a regular basis. This was about sixteen years ago, and to this day we still love our monthly card nights. We value this time together so much that we made it a priority by purposely scheduling it. As a matter of fact, each December my girlfriend and I take out our calendars and write in the next full year of card nights. That way we know it's on the calendar and won't get forgotten or overlooked in the midst of everything else we have going.

I believe that this card night story offers a valuable lesson. When we live busy lives, time can so easily slip away from us without us even realizing it. That is why if something is really important to me, I make a point of scheduling time for it. Doing this is my attempt at dedicating time to the people and events that I value most. I invite you to take a moment to ponder the things in your life that are most important to you. Is it spending quality time with friends and loved ones and/or doing certain activities? As you ponder your priorities, did you remember to include yourself in this list? Once your priorities are identified, I encourage you to treat them as such by specifically allotting time for them in your schedule. By contemplating our values and then scheduling the things that are of most importance, it allows us to take more control over the allocation of our time. This way we can ultimately create the desired balance that we wish to experience in our lives.

When I think of examples that I have implemented in my own life several come to mind. When my kids were little, after the tasks of the evening had been completed, scheduled into our routine was always about an hour of watching something on television together. This was enjoyable family time, but it also helped them to wind down before bedtime. Way back then we often had fun checking out movies and shows from the library, so we always had a variety of things to watch. As an advocate of education, I always jumped at the opportunity to rent something kid-oriented that would also teach them something. They still laugh together when they reminisce about some of the programs we used to watch that taught them social skills such as manners. Looking back, they probably were pretty cheesy videos, but the kids loved them at the time, and the morals instilled in them were positive. The library also had many seasons of a television series called *Little House on the Prairie* which was a show I had watched as a little girl. My kids became interested in it as well, and soon "Little House" was a regular in our home during TV time. One of my fondest memories is what they would do together while the credits were rolling and the ending song was playing. In their little onesie jammies, they would stand side by side in front of the TV and hop back and forth on their little dancing feet. Was I aware that this was their attempt at delaying bedtime as long as possible? Of course, but a slight delay in bedtime was a small price to pay for seeing the joy on their faces as they performed their dance for me as well as the priceless home videos I now have to remember those times.

Scheduled game nights with my kids are another thing that provided us with fun quality time together. Not only did it strengthen the bond between us, those fond memories will also last a lifetime. Now that they are much older, they usually turn me down when I suggest a game night, and instead suggest other things they would rather us do together. Even though my kids seem to have grown out of our game nights (at least for now), I know that this doesn't happen with every family. I know one particular family with college kids who still frequently have family game nights, often with the inclusion of friends. They all seem so happy and close, and I admire them as a strong family unit. Perhaps the day will come when my kids will embrace games at the kitchen table once again. I know they still play monopoly with their dad, so that's some wonderful quality time they have with him. With me they usually suggest watching a movie or show together, so we schedule times to do this. My son is currently home more than his sister so in-person movie time is more common with him at the moment. However, wherever she may be, my daughter still has access to our recorded shows via an app; she will often ask to schedule a time that we can watch something we enjoy together. We text each other when we have it cued up and pause after each segment to discuss. Once we have the next segment cued up, one of us will text, "go," and then we both press "play" simultaneously. I really enjoy this time with her, and doing this together makes us feel connected even though she's not physically in the house. When she *is* home, another tradition we started years ago is scheduling *Movie Mornings*. This is when we both commit to getting up early, meeting in the family room at a set time, making coffee and hot cocoa, and watching a movie together. I know I am likely different than most, but I don't generally have the time or attention span to watch an entire movie from start to finish unless it's in a theatre. Movie mornings however are an exception to this because this is time that has been specifically scheduled for us to spend together watching a movie of her choice.

Since I am fortunate enough to be close with all of my family, extended-family time is also a priority to me. Holidays are a given. Any of us within driving distance always make plans to celebrate together. For years the gathering place was my family's farm. It is a beautiful home, and we created so many years of wonderful memories there. I reminisce fondly about sitting in the solarium catching up with each other's lives, having wine tastings, and embracing the opportunity to commune together. Solarium time was always followed by a culinary masterpiece at the dining room table, coupled with entertaining stories and conversations. Eventually, the hosting torch was passed on to me, and I embrace it fully. My family is always welcome at my home for holiday meals and celebrations, and our time together here is as enjoyable as it has always been.

Another scheduled priority through the years has been to attend a tailgate and football game with my dad at a local university. For several years I could only do one a year because my kids had band competitions that conflicted with almost all of the games. As it usually turned out, one of the last games would work out once the kids' competitions came to an end. This past year my son was in the drumline of the university band. This made game days even more exciting for all of us. I made a point to put all of the home games on my calendar this year, and it was such a blessing getting to see my son and spend time with my dad and brother so frequently.

Years ago when my dad and step-mom bought their farm, they had an in-ground pool put in, something my dad had always wanted. A college student at the time, I would sometimes take a friend out there with me to enjoy an afternoon of swimming and sunbathing. Afternoon visits eventually evolved into something we would call *Pool Trips*. I had an agreement with my dad and stepmom that I could invite whomever I wanted because, for the most part, everyone slept outside in either a camper or a tent. It was basically a weekend-long camping trip with the privilege of bathrooms and showers. Everyone would bring their own food and drinks, and we were allowed to use the grill to barbeque our food. We would play music, swim, eat, drink, dance, and socialize all weekend. It was a perfect opportunity to spend time with family *and* friends, and we would schedule them three times each summer, rain or shine. If it rained we would sit around in the gazebo, visit, and play games. Some of the crazier friends would even swim in the rain as long as there was no thunder or lightning. I remember many an evening sitting on the old screened-in porch watching the light show in the sky during a summer thunderstorm, and one particular friend used to set up his air mattress out there and sleep all night.

Each pool trip took on a life of its own, each one different yet equally fun. Such a wide variety of people have attended over the years, some for the entire weekend and others for just a day's visit. There have been bonfires, hors d'oeuvres contests, and a numerous variety of musical jam sessions. These varied from my brother entertaining us with his guitar and vocals out by the pool, my father or daughter serenading us on the piano, to us bringing instruments and setting up a full band to perform on the deck. My brother would bring his bass guitar when he was visiting and jam endlessly with our father on the piano. My dear friend who plays percussion and steel drums often schedules her summer trips to the east coast around our pool trip dates. Many times she would bring her steel drums to be tuned in the area and then grace us with her amazing island steel drum music.

There was even an unforgettable weekend scene by the pool one year when an old friend had a little too much to drink. What appeared to us to come out of the blue, this person picked a fight with her boyfriend and quickly escalated from zero to sixty. She then proceeded to make her rounds yelling at us all. She told us each what she didn't like about us while we stared at her in disbelief and confusion. I still remember the look on my father's face as he looked up from his newspaper over his reading glasses, mouth wide open not knowing quite what to make of the fiasco he was witnessing. She concluded her episode by storming off in her bikini, leaving the property, and walking down the shoulder of a busy road. I'm not sure where she thought she was going, but of course, our men followed her in their vehicle and eventually convinced her to get in.

When they arrived back at the farm her boyfriend promptly took her home.

Later that evening we all sat around the bonfire uncharacteristically speechless while happy party music blared in contrast to the solemn mood that lingered in the air. I still chuckle when I think of this because the music had been prerecorded to adjust to the moods of the day and evening as the hours progressed. Island-type music accompanied the daytime, while more upbeat music played at night to match the usual Saturday night party vibe. Mishaps often make the best stories to be savored in the future, and I don't think a pool trip has gone by when this one hasn't gotten retold.

I spent my young adult years loving these pool trips, and several of us have since raised our children participating in this wonderful tradition. It has presented such an enjoyable opportunity for precious time with family and friends. I could probably write a whole separate book about our various pool trip weekends, but the point is that they continued year after year because we made it a priority to schedule them.

I am fortunate enough to have a timeshare in Mexico which has provided me with many opportunities to schedule quality time with family and friends, from annual family vacations to time with various friends who have come to join us. A cousin of mine whom I rarely get to see has already penciled in a week next year when he can join me on one of these getaways. Each year I look forward to scheduling the next trip whether with family, friends, or a combination of both. One year I even spent a week alone there, and I enjoyed it so much that I plan to do it again one day.

Another way that I schedule valuable time with friends is to schedule lunches or dinners with them. I have several people whom I refer to as lifetime friends. These are the friends whose friendship has lasted over the years and will undoubtedly continue for a lifetime. It doesn't matter how much time passes between visits, we always pick up right where we left off, as if we had seen each other just yesterday. I remember attending a scheduled lunch with one such friend, and since my then-boyfriend had never met or heard about her, he actually questioned whether she even existed.

One particular girlfriend and I came to the realization that when we get together to catch up over dinner at our favorite restaurant, if a few weeks have gone by, there is far too much to catch up on, and we inevitably visit way longer than anticipated. To avoid this we agreed to schedule these dinners on a weekly basis. Best decision ever! They came to be referred to as *Girlfriend Tuesdays,* and they are one of my biggest self-care practices. We both look forward to them, and usually one of us will start the conversation off with something along the lines of, "Wow, I needed this." Generally speaking, women are social beings, and for this reason, I feel that girlfriend conversations are invaluable. While guys tend to bond over a mutual activity, women are content simply talking and sharing with one another.

Each week I look forward to our scheduled dinners. It is therapeutic to share our various life experiences and either appreciate the satisfaction of some validation, or experience growth from being led to see things from another perspective. We have discussed a million different topics, from appreciating our guys and how they put up with our ever-changing moods and preferences, to venting our frustrations and brainstorming solutions. We are fairly like-minded and tend to vocalize more positives than negatives which usually results in feelings of contentment, appreciation, and/or inspiration.

I will never forget one particular conversation which occurred at a time when we were both in a good place, and she had many huge successes happening in her life. Regarding them, I distinctly remember her saying something along the lines of, "…and all I have been doing is having fun and playing in dirt," (i.e., gardening). How is it that when we relax and simply have fun, things tend to have a way of working out? Although this conversation was only a small blip on the radar of our *Girlfriend Tuesdays*, it still sticks with me to this day.

Do we complain also? I would love to say no, but we are human and sometimes just need to vent. However, we are aware enough to recognize that once we finish venting, it is time to let it go. Sometimes we laugh at our mishaps while enjoying each other's company and laughing at the irony of life. Through the years I have looked forward to and been grateful for these *Girlfriend Tuesdays*; I always leave them with my self-care cup feeling a little fuller than it was when I arrived.

Equally as important as my time with friends and loved ones is my time for solitude. Being an introvert, I need ample time alone to recharge. This means that my alone time is not only cherished, it is essential to my self-care practice. This leads me to a topic I refer to as *me-time*, time that is deliberately scheduled to be true to your authentic self and do whatever it is that you feel like doing. If you could have a day all to yourself with nothing on your "to-do" list, how would you spend it? I like to plan *me-time* for reading and writing. These are two of my favorite hobbies that often get neglected due to the plethora of domestic tasks, projects, and chores that are required to maintain a household and raise a family. As mentioned earlier, I do manage to sneak in *stolen moments* of time in my routines for reading. However, I realized at one point that I desired more time for reading and writing in my life, and if I really wanted it to happen, I would need to make it a priority and schedule it.

Being a ten-month employee, I am fortunate to have several weeks off each summer. One would think that would make it easy for me to read and write all the time. Think again. It's as if the free time creates a vacuum that instantly becomes filled with appointments, educational trainings, family get-togethers, parenting, yardwork, housework, meal prep, and so forth. For this reason, I made a commitment to myself to schedule a *me* day once a week all summer. I think of them as my reading/writing days, and I mark them on my calendar by drawing a heart.

If a conflict occurs on one of these days, I make a point to reschedule it. With that being said, I admittedly still find it a challenge to fully follow through with my summer reading/writing days each week. Therefore, as I write these words I am recommitting myself to improve upon this.

A *me-day* is basically a free day where I give myself "permission" to read and/or write as long as I feel like it with no guilt. If I have an inspiration to do something else, that is "allowed" as well, although chore lists are discouraged as they defeat the purpose of this day. On some *me* days, I enjoy wearing a summer sundress to help me feel pretty and feminine, while on others I strive only for comfort. I simply go with the flow of how I feel. Reminiscing about previous reading/writing days makes me crave and look forward to more, as they are such a gift to one's self.

I know some who have *me* days every Sunday, although they may not refer to them as such. They tell me that they get all of their chores and tasks finished on Saturday so that Sunday they can do nothing but relax. One friend said he likes planning *guy* days on Sundays to do nothing but watch sports. My cousin calls these days *Sunday Fundays.* Although I have not yet managed to complete everything on Saturday, leaving Sunday completely free, those who have inspire me that it *is* possible and that I shouldn't be limiting my *me* time to summers only.

Ultimately, one day a week such as Sunday would be ideal, but if I can't yet manage to take a complete Sunday for myself, I can certainly begin with baby steps by *leaning into it.* That being said, I am setting the intention now to at least schedule *me* blocks of time each week. This will ideally consist of three to four hours of time set aside on a Sunday to read, write, or do whatever the heck I want to do, as it might vary from time to time. How about you? Will you commit with me? *Me-time* and *me* days are excellent ways to exercise self-care. Your time may be similar or completely different than mine since people have such a wide variety of preferences. How you spend it is up to you. The point is to schedule time for ourselves that is planned and built into our daily or weekly lives. Think about it. How can you prioritize and schedule some *me-time* into your own life? It is something that we all need and deserve. Let's do this!

Chapter Seven

PRIORITIES, BOUNDARIES, AND BALANCE

"To thine own self be true" is a famous Shakespearian quote that I feel is noteworthy. I recall an old college friend telling me how important it is to always be true to yourself. I am not sure that I even knew what those words meant back then, but today I most definitely do, and I strive to live by them. When I ponder the meaning of being true to one's self, the word *congruence* comes to mind, congruence with the inner self and the outer self. One way of gauging this is by asking yourself the following question, "Is what I am choosing to do consistent with my inner values?" I can't stress enough the importance of being in alignment with your own principles and remaining faithful to your core values. Noticing how you feel when you think about doing something provides great insight. If you don't feel good about a particular decision, perhaps that is your intuition guiding you away from something that would not be in harmony with your authentic self.

Try writing out your most cherished beliefs and values, for this is the core of who you are and what you should consistently strive to represent via your actions and behaviors. What are the things that are most important to you? This is a question worth exploring, for the answer should guide your daily decisions. As previously stated, if there is something that you enjoy doing, make it a priority to do it on a regular basis. At the same time, consider giving up things that are not in alignment with your beliefs and desires. This is a way of claiming ownership of your life and molding it to suit your current preferences.

If someone asks you to commit to an obligation, listen to your gut for the answer. If you feel good about doing it, great. Then do it. On the other hand, if it would take precious time away from your priorities such as family time etc., it's okay to say no. That is part of taking care of yourself and staying true to your priorities. Yes, of course, care for others. Just don't do so at the expense of not properly taking care of yourself.

This brings me to the topic of boundaries which are a major part of self-care practice. After years of getting burned for not respecting mine as I should have, I have come to realize the immensity of their value. Your personal boundaries determine what is okay to you and what is not okay to you. Physical boundaries have to do with your own personal space and level of comfort around others. Knowing this about yourself can lead you to speak up if someone is making you feel uncomfortable physically. Mental boundaries are utilized when you decide whether to say yes or no to something. Emotional boundaries pertain to the level of personal feelings and emotions you are willing to share with someone, which may in part be determined by the level of trust and intimacy you share. Emotional boundaries also have to do with how you expect to be treated by others. If someone treats you in a way that is not acceptable to you, it is your right to speak up. They say we teach others how to treat us, and our boundaries assist us in doing this. If someone isn't respecting your boundaries, they are not respecting you. Just remember that you always have the option of removing someone from your experience as a means of protecting and respecting yourself. Know who you are and what you prioritize, determine your boundaries, and remain true to yourself by honoring them.

Be firm with your boundaries as necessary, but also know that it is okay to be flexible with them when appropriate. An example would be agreeing to serve on a committee at work in spite of a lack of interest in doing so. A reason may be that you value your job enough to recognize that if it is important to your boss and/or coworkers, perhaps you should be willing to step up and do your part. Another example is when a loved one wants to do something together that isn't on your list of desirable activities. There are times when we do things simply because we love someone and want to nurture the relationship. How many men have sat in a mall chair waiting for their wives to shop? An innumerable amount, I am sure. I know of countless parents and relatives who attend event after event, whether it be sports or otherwise because they love and want to support and encourage a child. How many parties or events have you participated in for the sole reason that you knew it meant a lot to someone and you wanted to show your support? These are all healthy examples of things we do because we value our relationships, and they beautifully represent basic human kindness. Determine the boundaries that are most important to you as well as when is it okay to make exceptions. As long as you are not sacrificing yourself and your own self-care, then there is nothing wrong with accommodating the needs and desires of others. In fact, loving, helping, and supporting other people is one of the most gratifying and rewarding things we can do.

Honoring priorities and boundaries helps us to create balance in our lives, which is an important part of self-care practice. When my children were small, I yearned for the balance of downtime after a busy day of working and tending to my kids. A parenting tip from my mom afforded me the opportunity to achieve such balance. Her advice was to have a nightly routine with my children that includes a 7:00 bedtime. This boundary provided me with time to do whatever tasks I needed to do without interruptions as well as time to wind down prior to turning in for the night. This simple bedtime advice turned out to be invaluable. For my children, it provided a predictable routine that made them feel secure. For me, it provided a nightly opportunity for self-care and balance.

Be cognizant of your core values, and honor your priorities. Then set healthy boundaries as needed in order to create a comfortable balance between responsibilities and self-care.

Chapter Eight

JOURNALING

Journaling can be a valuable tool for self-care, and there are numerous ways to participate. Some enjoy documenting their daily experiences. This can be done regularly in the form of a diary or as a way to capture special moments and adventures, such as a travel journal. Many have written memoirs of their life experiences, the lessons they have learned along the way, and the personal growth they have experienced as a result of their journey. This can be done simply for self-expressive purposes or with the intention of sharing with others. There are many among us who have a story to tell, whether it be for the purpose of helping others, documenting history, or simply for entertainment.

Journaling can also be a powerful tool for expressing and processing thoughts and emotions. It can be cathartic to let go of pent-up emotions by writing them down. Sometimes people have feelings about a person or situation that they cannot express verbally for one reason or another. A private journal can be a safe place for releasing these feelings.

One of my favorite forms of journaling is freewriting. This was illustrated in the poem I shared in this book's introduction. With freewriting, one simply puts pen to paper and writes freely. This is an excellent way to process feelings and emotions, bring out your creativity, and connect with your inner self. Some of my best writing has been via freewriting, and it is the most profound feeling when it occurs. I remember writing countless lyrics while listening to live music at a local nightclub. The band would drown out the thoughts in my head, allowing me to focus solely on the music, while at the same time my hand would travel feverishly across the pages of my journal, writing some of my best lyrical creations. It was as if the words were downloaded from above directly to my fingers as raw emotions were splattered over the pages with words, void of interference from my conscious mind. If you haven't tried freewriting, I would suggest giving it a try sometime. It is a wonderful way to create a sense of self-connection, and who knows, you may discover that you're more creative than you think.

Another favorite journaling technique is keeping a gratitude journal. As discussed previously, appreciation is powerful. Writing about things you are grateful for is a wonderful way of elevating your mood and emotions. It's incredible how well this works, and I have experienced it firsthand on many occasions. In my counseling practice, it is astonishing to observe the almost immediate shift in the spirits of my students when I am able to get them to speak about things they appreciate. It becomes evident in their posture, their tone of voice, and their facial expressions. Challenge yourself to write down at least five things a day for which you are grateful. Look around and appreciate the small stuff, and you will find that there is an abundance from which to choose. I encourage everyone to keep a gratitude journal and enjoy its many benefits.

Another way to journal that is highly effective is to keep a journal of your goals and desires. This is where you write not only about what you want but also why you want it, for there is something mysteriously powerful that lies within the *why* behind your dreams. It is also helpful to include the feelings you wish to experience once your goal is achieved. Writing about your goals and desires is an effective way to focus your mind on the direction you want to go in life. As you write about these goals and desires, thoughts about them become more active in your consciousness and your awareness. Neurons will connect in your brain which will in turn allow these positive thoughts to flow more freely and frequently in the future. This journal acts as a powerful tool to support the visualization process and the momentum of positive experiences. As you describe your desired outcome, you can be as general or as specific as you like. Write freely. If it feels good when you think about it, write it down and describe it in detail. If it feels unrealistic or unattainable, try being more general in your description and focusing on how you want to feel, because at the route of your desire is how you expect to feel when it is obtained. Is it appreciation that you are ultimately seeking, or is it the feeling of freedom you would experience from the choices and opportunities your desired outcome would bring you? Whatever it is, focus on that and write about it. A goal and desire journal is another powerful and uplifting way to use journaling in your self-care practice.

Lastly, my workbook entitled *Fill Your Cup Daily Journal* is an excellent tool for implementing the ideas presented in this book. It includes morning and evening sentence starters intended to assist you in purposefully focusing your thoughts to improve your general mood, feelings, and daily experiences. It provides an excellent means for shaping your day, living your life on purpose, and experiencing more joy and gratitude.

Chapter Nine

COMPARTMENTALIZING: A Helpful Strategy for Managing a Busy Schedule while Still Keeping Your Sanity

Juggling the countless responsibilities of life can be difficult, often leaving little time for self-care. Over the years, I have realized how important self-care is to physical, mental, and emotional well-being by observing the toll that neglecting it took on myself and others around me. This is why throughout this book I have shared ideas and suggestions for including self-care in your routine. However, let's face it. Sometimes our numerous responsibilities can feel overwhelming, especially if you think about them all at once. This leads me to introduce a time-management technique that has helped me immensely. I refer to it as *compartmentalizing.* In order to implement this strategy, allot specific times for devoting your undivided attention to the different aspects of your life. This may include work, school & homework, family time, self-care time, or any number of other activities. For example, when you are at work, focus all of your attention on your work tasks, while resisting the temptation to think about all of the things you need to do afterward. Similarly, when you are having family time or self-care time, don't spend it worrying about all that you have to do for work or school. Focusing on all of your responsibilities at once can be paralyzing and cause you to feel overwhelmed. This in turn may result in procrastination, and can even lead to a mental breakdown. For this reason, I recommend compartmentalizing to help manage your daily tasks and responsibilities.

During a recent conversation with my son, I was delighted when he described how he is compartmentalizing his own life in order to manage his rigorous college schedule. He is a civil engineering major with demanding honors classes, each requiring an extensive amount of time and devotion. In addition, he participates in musical ensembles that require large time commitments as well as private practice on his instrument. During our conversation over dinner, I was thrilled to hear how he is compartmentalizing his time for the benefit of his productivity, success, and mental wellbeing. He shared that when he's doing his music, he focuses only on that, and when he's attending classes or doing homework, he thinks only about the current task at hand. He said that often he will work extra hard to finish his homework early in order to have some time for relaxing afterward. On other days, he schedules homework, takes breaks to relax, and then hits the books once again. One of his favorite self-care activities is going to the gym and shooting hoops with "the guys." He told me that during this block of time, he tells himself not to think about anything except enjoying playing ball. What a healthy thing for him to do! Not only is he doing something he loves while not letting it interfere with his goals and responsibilities, he has an outlet for his emotions and daily stressors. This is coupled with the health benefits that come with any form of exercise.

Throughout the stages of my life, I too have experienced a variety of demanding schedules. Out of all of them, the biggest challenge I have faced with managing my time and my sanity was when I went back to school to get my school counseling degree. My children were two and four years old at the time, and I was working full time during the day, while attending classes and doing schoolwork in the evenings. My then-husband's work schedule kept him out until at least the kids' bedtime, so on nights when I had class, I had to hire a babysitter. It was a strenuous year and a half, to say the least, and I don't know how I could have made it all work without purposely compartmentalizing the things I needed to do. I gave each of my responsibilities their own allotted time and space in my schedule. My rule of thumb was that when I was at work, I had to focus my attention solely on work. When I was with the kids or family, I would focus only on them and what they needed. For the blocks of time after they went to bed, as well as some hours set aside on weekends, I would focus completely on school work. If I would have thought about all of these responsibilities at once, I think my head might have exploded. I would have driven myself crazy, frozen like a deer in headlights, unable to get anything done due to stress and anxiety. As it turns out, being disciplined with compartmentalizing enabled me to be successful at obtaining the degree that paved the road to my dream job, while also maintaining my current occupation and enjoying raising my family. Would I want to take on a schedule like that again at my age? The answer is a clear *absolutely not*. However, I do recognize the value that period of time had on improving my family's lifestyle, and I am grateful that I was able to use this tool to help me successfully achieve my goal.

How do I use compartmentalizing now? Much in the same way. When I am at my job, I give 100% to work. Once I leave for the day, I leave it behind until I return the next day. This way when I am home, I am free to focus my full attention on my domestic responsibilities and activities. Taking my focus off of work during this time also allows me the opportunity to recharge so that I am able to give 100% again the following day. Is this possible all of the time? Of course not. Naturally there are exceptions, but for the most part, I follow these general guidelines.

Regarding the goal of leaving work behind at the end of the day, this brings me to recognize a particular challenge that comes into play for those who work in any sort of caregiving role. As caregivers, we are genuinely concerned about the well-being of our students, patients, and/or clients. If we weren't, we wouldn't have chosen this profession. Because we care so much, it can be difficult for us not to worry about the ones we serve during our leisure hours. However, consider this. What does worrying about them while you're not at work do for them? Nothing. What does it do for you? It robs you of your opportunity to rest and refill your tank so that you can go back the next day refreshed and ready to serve once again. Don't get me wrong, if I felt for one minute that devoting time to worrying about my students would help them in any way, it would be worth allotting time for worrying about them. However, the reality is that I cannot worry enough about my students to make a difference in their lives. All I can do is take care of myself when I am not with them so that when I see them again, I am replenished and ready to be the best I can be for them.

When I first began trying to mentally and emotionally let work go when leaving my job for the day, I was a teacher who found this very difficult to do. The kids weighed so heavily on my heart, and I wondered how I could possibly let my thoughts of them go for any amount of time. Still, I realized that it would be healthier for my family and for me if I could. The way I finally found success was through the use of visualization when it was time to go home. I would imagine that I had a work coat on my back filled with all of my students' baggage and all of my concern for them. Before leaving for the day, I would visualize myself physically taking off this coat and dropping it behind me to be left at work. Sometimes it felt like the coat was so heavy it was sticking to me, and I would have to shake it off. However, I began doing this daily, and it really helped me begin setting boundaries between my job and my personal life. After all, each is its own compartment and should be treated accordingly.

I encourage you to ponder ways that you can incorporate compartmentalizing, as it is a great tool for honoring each aspect of your life by giving it the undivided attention it deserves.

Chapter Ten

RELATIONSHIPS

Despite being an introvert who needs and loves solitude, relationships with others are extremely important to me. From my closest relationships with family and friends, to my acquaintances, to random people and strangers I see or interact with each day, I see value in all of them. As humans, we are social beings who have a natural desire for a sense of belonging and connecting with others. The people you surround yourself with have a tremendous effect on your life, so it's important to choose them wisely and then nurture those relationships accordingly. Notice that I said *relationships* as opposed to *relationship, for* a healthy support system should ideally consist of more than one person. This way when one of them is not physically or emotionally available, you have someone else to connect with or confide in. It can also be helpful to get more than one person's perspective on any issues you may face, for everyone sees the world through their own lens. Understand and accept that we all need help and support at some point in our lives, and we can be either the giver or the receiver of that support depending on the situation.

I feel blessed that I have a wonderful support system of both family and friends. I talk to a few on a regular or semi-regular basis. With others, our encounters may be less frequent, but the general theme is that when we do talk or visit with one another, it's like no time has passed since our last interaction, and we pick up right where we left off. I refer to the friends in this category as my *lifetime friends*. I catch up with my lifetime friends and family in a few ways depending on who it is and the surrounding situation, and of course, I connect with any of them on an as-needed basis if someone is in need of support. With some friends and family, we schedule gatherings and visits as time allows and when events come up such as holidays, barbeques, birthdays, etc. I have a few other lifetime friends that I meet for lunch or dinner whenever we decide to schedule it. Often I catch up with them on a day after work or when one of them happens to be in the area. Usually, it begins with a text such as this, "Hey, when can we meet for lunch to catch up? It's been too long," and then we put something on the calendar. I invite you to think about your own confidants and assure that you are doing your part to maintain those relationships. After all, having a strong social support system is a key factor in self-care.

Harmony and Conflict in Relationships

I have heard the description of "people pleaser" used with negative connotations. However, I am going to offer another perspective. I would describe it as making a conscious choice to take the path of least resistance whenever possible. As an admitted people pleaser, if I can have a harmonious social interaction without sacrificing my boundaries or values, that is my preference. In most cases, I see no point in participating in unnecessary conflict if it can be avoided. I do this fairly effortlessly with strangers and acquaintances, as I see no need to delve deep into personal beliefs that could potentially expose contrary opinions. After all, why choose to focus on differences when I can so easily focus on similarities? Everyone has feelings, needs, and basic human desires, and most have one or more people whom they love dearly. The majority of individuals are generally well-meaning at their core, and their natural inclination is to help someone in need. Call me old-fashioned in this crazy world we live in, but I truly believe in the basic goodness of humanity, and that at the center of all of us, is love. Imagine someone falling down and dropping all of their things in public. I can almost guarantee that at least one person and more than likely multiple people will step in to lend a hand, for that is the kind of human nature that I both observe and choose to direct my focus.

Just as there are two sides to every coin, it would be remiss of me not to acknowledge some exceptions to my harmonious tendencies, as there are times when conflict is necessary. For example, it is often unavoidable when setting a new boundary or correcting wrongdoing, and many positive changes have been made in our world because of people who were willing to face conflict in the name of the righteousness of their cause.

We live in a diverse world with a plethora of personalities and opinions, and this vast variety is what makes our world what it is. I have a friend who was captain of a debate team, and she loves a heated discussion consisting of opposing viewpoints. She gets excited and emotionally charged when involved in such conversations. Look around, it is not difficult to find others who get this same pleasure from arguing their point. Lawyers, politicians, and television commentators are just a few of numerous examples. I have sat around many a table enjoying the energy exchange of people stressing valid points of opposing opinions. When done amicably and respectfully without hitting below the belt (I am told this is called *Rules of Engagement* in debating), these conversations can be not only stimulating but absolutely fascinating.

Another example of useful or productive conflict is regarding those in your inner-most circles, such as someone you live with, your children, a significant other, or anyone with whom you have a deeper, more intimate connection. Although there may be times in these relationships where the avoidance of conflict is the best choice at that moment, habitually avoiding conflict can lead to misunderstandings, built-up resentment, and a lack of depth in the connection you share. As mentioned above, it is much easier to make the choice of avoiding conflict with strangers and acquaintances because it is not necessary that you know everything about each other in order to experience a mutually positive interaction. However, in our closest, most intimate relationships, addressing conflicts can be an integral part of strengthening understanding, making mutually satisfying agreements, finding resolutions, and ultimately bringing more depth to the connection.

Relationships are an integral part of life and socialization. I appreciate and honor the variety of human connections that I get to experience in my life. From the baby who makes eye contact with me in the store as we share an innocent smile, to the students and families I am honored to serve, to my acquaintances, co-workers, and those nearest and dearest to my heart, I value and appreciate each one of them and their part in my life. Creating and maintaining harmony with others can bring immense peace and satisfaction, and therefore, is another form of self-care.

Your Nearest and Dearest

Tomorrow is not promised, a saying that can be carelessly forgotten until it is too late. I urge you to avoid such a tragedy by maintaining peace in your closest relationships when at all possible. I always tell my kids and family members that I love them before we part ways or hang up the phone because it is important to my heart that every exchange ends with an affirmation of my love for them. It is vitally important not to take for granted the loved ones in our lives. I encourage you to frequently share your feelings of love and appreciation with those who are most precious to you. This is a way of avoiding the possibility of painful guilt and regret in the future, and instead, creating a sense of inner peace, knowing that you left no important words unsaid. Make that overdue apology, express your gratitude, and say "thank you" to someone who has supported you in some way. Hug your children, your parents, your spouse, etc. When we recognize and acknowledge that tomorrow is not promised, we gain a deeper appreciation for the precious time we are blessed to have with our most cherished family and friends.

People all Around

   People are everywhere. It's difficult to avoid them, and being the social creatures that we are, most wouldn't want to. They are fellow shoppers and employees at the store, diners and wait staff at a restaurant, drivers and passengers in traffic, and coworkers and clients at work. Mr. Rogers referred to them as *the people in your neighborhood*, and he set a wonderful example of showing appreciation and kindness to all. Regardless of the role they might currently have in your experience, it is important to remember and acknowledge that they are all people who deserve to be valued and treated with respect, whether you have anything in common with them or not. For example, I don't have any interest in or knowledge of plumbing, but I am grateful that there are people who do. Similarly, I have no interest in caring for the sick or tending to wounds, but fortunately for all of us, there are many who do. Our various personalities, talents, and skillsets are what make the world go 'round. It is also important to remember that the people you see and encounter in your daily experiences have their own emotions, struggles, and challenges. They likely have families who love and count on them. The fact is, we usually don't have any idea what a stranger or acquaintance has been through or might be currently going through. Don't be the person who causes further hurt or despair in someone when you could just as easily be a bright spot in their day by striving to be an up-lifter. They say that a good way to judge someone's true character is not by how they treat you when they are wanting to impress, but instead by how they treat their waiter, the person who serves them at the drive-through, and strangers in general.

   My father sets a beautiful example of how to treat the people you come into contact with throughout your day. When I accompany him on errands or excursions of any kind, he makes small talk with everyone with whom he interacts. He always asks how they are doing, and if it's someone he sees on a regular basis (such as the bank teller or local merchant) he always asks and remembers their name so that he can address them accordingly. This is how we all should strive to be. When I am successful at this, I not only feel good about myself, I get more fulfillment from my experiences. When people are treated with respect and kindness, their tendency is usually to reciprocate, thus contributing to a more peaceful and loving community.

Have you ever noticed something positive about someone without voicing it? Perhaps they look nice or have nicely done nails or hair, or maybe they are especially kind, dependable, or helpful at work. Whatever the case, I encourage you to be generous with your compliments. If I think something nice about someone, no matter how small, I try to make a point of voicing it to them. Why keep these thoughts to yourself when you could use them to brighten someone's day? As mentioned above, we don't know what someone may be going through, and a kind word or compliment may be just what they need to hear. When I do this, I find that I not only usually prompt a smile, I also feel uplifted by the satisfaction of sharing human benevolence.

Difficult People

In a perfect world, everyone would think before they speak and treat each other with respect and kindness. However, at one point or another, we all find ourselves in the company of difficult people. Let's face it, sometimes people are rude. While we cannot control how other people act, it behooves us to contemplate and intentionally decide how we will react to them, not only behaviorally, but also with our internal dialogue.

While raising my children, I would attempt to reframe their initial reaction to someone behaving poorly. I would tell them that watching their rude behavior makes me feel grateful that I was raised to have better manners than that. I would express that I feel sorry they were not taught to be kinder. Sometimes I would say something like, "They look pretty angry and miserable. I am glad I am not feeling the way they must be feeling right now."

Sometimes it's important to give others the benefit of the doubt, whether you feel they deserve it or not. After all, most people are doing the best they can with what they have, and some are better at social skills than others. Perhaps they are in a bad marriage or are dealing with a difficult challenge. These are all things of which you would likely be unaware. Even if their behavior towards you is poor, remember that your response to them is not about them but rather a reflection of yourself. Know your own character, and to that remain true. This way at the end of the day you will be able to look yourself in the mirror and know that you acted in accordance with your own values based on the person you want to be.

Not everyone experienced an ideal upbringing, and those displaying rude, angry behaviors, are likely feeling strong, negative emotions as opposed to contentment or happiness. For this reason, I encourage you to observe poorly behaving people through a lens of compassion rather than judgment. In turn, feel appreciative that you are not experiencing the present moment in the same way that they are.

It is naturally much easier to feel compassion for someone when their rudeness is not directed at you. When it is, however, it becomes personal, and thinking objectively is much more challenging. Still, the reality is that sometimes in life we will, at least for a time, have to deal directly with a difficult person. How can we do this most effectively while also honoring our own self-care to the greatest extent possible? First, if someone doesn't make you feel good, focus on them as little as possible, remembering that what we focus on in life tends to increase in our experiences. For example, dealing with someone at work might be unavoidable, but stressing and complaining about them outside of work is a choice. Assuming that thoughts of them don't make you feel good, it can't possibly be beneficial for you to dedicate your personal time to focusing on the reasons you dislike them.

If you feel a strong need to vent in an effort to release the stress that they caused you, strive to do this as briefly as possible and then promptly let it go. Turn your thoughts to more pleasurable topics. After all, are they really worth sacrificing time and attention that could be better put elsewhere, such as towards loved ones or things that bring you joy? Remember, the things you choose to think about have a direct impact on how you feel and what you experience.

There was a person who used to continually tell me horror stories about how someone at work would go out of their way to undermine him at any opportunity. After listening and validating his feelings with compassion, my response became something like this, "Is this person really worth so much of your attention and energy? He's not even here right now, and yet you are letting him dominate your thoughts and becoming increasingly annoyed as you do." My message was basically that if you don't like him, take your attention away from him when he is not in your direct experience. There are plenty of other people and things to focus on that are much more pleasant. My point was understood, received, and put into practice; and guess what? A short time later the culprit left the department and now their paths never cross.

When you do have to interact with difficult people in your life, try to find *something* positive about them (no matter how difficult that may be), and focus as much as you can on any admirable traits they may have. Are they nice occasionally? If so, put your focus on that. Maybe they have created a successful career for themselves, or they have nice taste in clothes. It can be anything, no matter the stretch. Just find something favorable about them to focus on any chance you get.

I have applied these strategies with multiple difficult or challenging people over the years. What I usually find happens over time, is they either change, or they go away. That sounds funny, but it's actually pretty amazing, and it has worked wonders in my life. Several examples come to mind of people who have either changed (my experience with them changed for the better) or gone away (our paths no longer cross). I have people whom I used to consider difficult, who are now wonderful to me and valuable in my life. I experience a whole different side of them than I used to, and it's awesome. Others have simply moved on for their own purposes and are no longer in my life. Have you ever said, "I would love my job if it weren't for that *one* person!"? Try this practice. Search for and highlight any positive qualities you can find, forget about them when they're not in your presence, and watch what happens over time.

In comparison to the saying, *Don't miss the forest for the trees*, it is also important to be careful not to *miss the message for the delivery*. Many times in various types of relationships I have felt initial resistance or hurt to what I took as criticism from another, only to later recognize a valid point in their position, following more open consideration. For example, if someone criticizes your work, perhaps they have a good eye for detail which could benefit you in the long run. Maybe they have a helpful point in there somewhere that you were unable to receive initially because of your natural instinct to feel defensive. The passage of a little time can do wonders for lowering defensiveness and allowing one to process and reconsider an initial reaction to someone's opinion. People's conversational skills vary widely. Therefore, it can be helpful to note that sometimes underneath a less-than-ideal delivery could be a message worth receiving.

In addition to the suggested strategies and considerations for dealing with difficult people, it is extremely important to understand and remember that your self-worth is not determined by others. Just because someone says something about you does not make it true. In fact, it says more about *them* than it does about you. Consider the wisdom in the phrase *What others think of you is none of your business*. The things people say about others are more of a reflection of who *they* are than a representation of whom they are speaking. For example, if someone is insulting another, they are portraying themselves as someone who, for whatever reason, has the need to put others down.

As I work with youth struggling with the words or opinions of others, I strive to help them understand this concept. One example that I use is to ask the student how they would feel if I told them they are covered in green stripes and orange polka dots, often making the statement to them directly. Almost always they laugh at the absurdity of my comment because they are unequivocally certain that it is false. I ask if what I said caused them to consider that it might actually be true, and they always say no. When I ask what they would think of me after making such an observation about them, the usual response is something along the lines of, *I think Mrs. Bryant may losing it, as she obviously cannot see me clearly.* I then encourage them to look at the insults of others in a similar manner, understanding that the comments essentially have nothing to do with them or who they are. I also work with the ones who have done the insulting, for they clearly have their own issues that need to be addressed. However, the point is that someone's value is not determined by the words of another, for each of us is a worthy being regardless of the words or actions of someone else.

While all of this is true, it is noteworthy here to recognize that children are particularly vulnerable to being hurt and even shaped by the words of others, especially the adults they look to for care and guidance. Our little ones come to us as innocent and impressionable beings, which puts an enormous amount of power and responsibility on those blessed with caring for them. They look to their parents and caregivers to help them develop their sense of self. They are easily influenced and often live up to the descriptions of themselves they hear adults making, albeit positive or negative. As you consider the interactions you have with others, especially children for the reasons aforementioned, I urge you to choose your words carefully because the impact they have can be far-reaching.

To reiterate strategies for dealing with difficult people, first attempt to see them through a lens of compassion, for you don't know what they may be going through. Assume that they are doing the best they can with what they have, even if their social skills are atrocious. When you are not with them, let them go from your mind, and focus instead on the things in your life that are important to you. Notice anything positive about them that you can find, and focus on these things when you are around them. Lastly, remember that their behavior is a reflection of them, and is not related in any way to your inherent value. What is most important as you apply these strategies, is that you feel better, both in and out of their presence.

Chapter Eleven

SELF-CARE IN THE LIVES OF OTHERS

When I asked multiple people about their favorite self-care practices, some common themes were music, creativity, movement, nature, gratitude, time management, and spirituality or religion.

Music seems to speak to everyone, as there is an abundance available for every mood, personality, and occasion. Music can be created, sung, played on an instrument, listened to, danced to, and used to create a mood or ambiance. One friend shared that she likes to play music and sing along during her breaks at work because it relieves stress and elevates her mood, regenerating her for the next phase of her day. Another friend turned her entire life around, from being homeless and humiliated, to owning her own land and home, raising beautiful children, working her dream job, going on adventures, and appreciating the beauty of everyday life. She attributes this miraculous turnaround to reuniting with and embracing her love of music and dancing. By doing this, she shifted her energy and mood so much that it created a new inspiration for life within her that propelled her toward the many positive things that came her way.

One time while traveling, I I noticed a phrase tattooed on a man's arm and inquired about its meaning. As it turns out, the words are song lyrics that are very symbolic to him. Sadly, at one point in his life, he felt suicidal. According to him, the phrase he wears on his arm are the very words that saved his life. He explained that when he listened, he felt like the song was speaking directly to him. The message in those lyrics is to choose life over death. He wears this tattoo as a reminder of all he has overcome, and most importantly, to remember to always choose life.

Equally therapeutic to listening to music is creating it. Expressing creativity of any kind is a wonderful form of self-care. One childhood and lifelong friend shared that creating and connecting with his muse on a regular basis was his self-care as a young adult. He went on to describe how feelings change, coming and going like the wind. "That's the beauty of the human condition," he says, sounding much like his wise and creative father. He recommends channeling these feelings into creation, whatever that means to you, art, music, words, dance, or any other form of creating.

When we speak of connecting with our creativity, we often think of the arts. However, creativity spans much wider than this. It can be seen in the engineer designing a bridge, in a business person embarking upon a project, or in a marketing team working on an advertising campaign. If you are involved in a creative project of any kind that inspires you, then as one person explained, you will always have something to look forward to. That inspiration, that drive to put your energy into something you are creating, is life flowing through you, keeping you forward-looking and purpose-driven.

Movement, nature, and positive thinking all came up frequently when speaking with others about their favorite self-care practices. Several people expressed that they enjoy taking a walk outside at lunchtime or at the beginning or end of the day, either alone or with a friend or loved one. Coworkers walking together at lunchtime was also suggested because it creates a habit, commitment, and accountability, not to mention a nice break in the day. One quick and simple thing a neighbor shared was that she enjoys nature by facing the view of the woods in her backyard while she brushes her teeth because it brings her peace. Another person described a practice that he likes to use right before he goes to bed. He focuses on his blessings and all that he has accomplished, allowing these positive thoughts to be what is at the forefront of his mind as he drifts off to sleep. What a wonderful way to not only enhance feelings of appreciation but also to assist in building and maintaining positive self-esteem.

Although I have addressed time management in multiple ways, when I asked one particular person how she manages all she does while also taking care of herself in the process, she shared something that I love. She recommends making it a priority to plan free time into your schedule, time to do whatever it is that you want to do at that moment. "Don't be working all the time," she said. Instead, have a block of time during your day when you don't have anything scheduled, no plans at all, even if ironically, you have to schedule it to be sure it doesn't get overlooked. When this time block occurs, you may choose to do anything you want or nothing at all, either one being a viable option. She expressed how having this time built into her days gives her a feeling of freedom and makes her feel like she has room to breathe. Don't we all desire that?

Spirituality and religion were other common themes that continued to come up as people shared their self-care practices and where they draw their strength. Whether it be via prayer, meditation, yoga, and/or attending religious services, the need for this connection was ever-present in their descriptions. As I pondered whom to ask about their self-care suggestions, one person stood out to me. I would describe her as calm and graceful, always emanating warmth and peace. She is usually smiling and quite frankly, she glows. She so eloquently encompassed prayer, faith, gratitude, movement, and mindfulness in her description of her personal self-care routine, that it is my pleasure and honor to close this chapter with the words of my dear friend.

My self-care begins and ends with prayer...a prayer of gratitude! I believe when we recognize that there is a higher power over us and in us we can never be defeated.

I have developed a consistent yoga practice...it didn't happen overnight. After prayer, I connect with myself through breathing and intentional movement. I need to feel my body, noticing what is uncomfortable and what feels good. A good stretch sets the tone for your posture and helps to incorporate confidence, flexibility, and balance as you go through the day.

When my sister died suddenly, I was broken and left with a huge responsibility to take in my mother and nephew. Things happened quickly, and I found that intentional walking alone, paying attention to the birds singing and the breeze/sun on my face helped clear my mind and build stamina to move forward.

My glow comes from being intentional with MYSELF through prayer, yoga, walking, and being with what is!!!!

Chapter Twelve

REFLECTION & CONCLUSION

Life is a precious journey, and you get to create it as you go. There will be goals you will strive for, but it is equally important to enjoy the moments along the way. Remember to be gentle with yourself, and that there is no one right path. We each get to carve our own way. If you find yourself on a pathway that you do not enjoy, reset your course, and try another direction, for each day presents the gift of a new beginning.

Sharing love with others in whatever capacity one chooses, begins with self-love and self-care. When you love and care for yourself, you can more fully and successfully love, care for, and support others. It is not a selfish thing, it is a human thing that we as a society have sadly allowed ourselves to deviate from.

Throughout this book, I have shared thoughts, ideas, and self-care practices that have worked for me and contributed immensely to the happiness I experience in my life. I hope that you will take whatever resonates with you and incorporate it into your own life, however you see fit. After all, we are all different in what makes us tick, and our variety as individuals, like the colors of a rainbow, is a beautiful thing. Be kind to yourself, and you will find that you are naturally more compassionate with others. Understand the immense value of self-care, and integrate it into your routines. Fill your cup *daily*, knowing that it is the greatest gift you can give to yourself as well as to anyone who is affected, influenced, or loved by you.

Acknowledgments

Writing a book turned out to be a much longer process than I had ever imagined. Ecstatic to have finally reached the finish line, there are several people for whom I am ever grateful. First and foremost, I would like to thank my publisher, Rebecca Benston, for her belief in this project from its infancy. I have been a lifetime writer and creator, but I am a new author. Rebecca has been encouraging, kind, and extremely patient with me throughout this journey. I cannot begin to express how much I have learned along the way. I am passionate about the importance of self-care, and releasing this book into the world makes me feel like one of my life's purposes is being fulfilled. Thank you, Rebecca, for blessing me with a voice in this industry and for allowing this book's message to be shared.

Next, I would like to thank my three editors, Frank Adkins, Stephanie Lehane, and Margo Zitin, whom all came forth voluntarily, each believing in this project and wanting to be supportive of its evolvement. Frank, my lifelong and cherished friend, thank you for your continued encouragement, for checking in often to see how things were progressing, and for offering to help in any way you could. Your initial notes literally made me a better writer, causing me to revisit the manuscript with fresh eyes. I don't know how you found the time with everything else that you do, but you made this project a priority and even drove the distance to hand-deliver your notes to me. Thank you. My second editor, Stephanie Lehane, is my brilliant and talented best friend. Thank you Steph, for taking time on our "girls' vacation" to read through chapters and write your wonderful editing suggestions. When you could have been relaxing in the pool, you dedicated your time to this book, and I appreciate that more than you know. Last, but certainly not least, I would like to thank Margo Zitin for offering a final set of eyes on this project before its release. Thank you Margo, for going above and beyond as you demonstrated your devotion. You bought a new printer for the sole purpose of printing out my book, overnighted me pages on more than one occasion, and even worked from a hospital bed when that was your temporary location. I cannot thank you enough. Frank, Steph, and Margo, this book would not be what it is without your support.

I would also like to thank all who shared their self-care ideas as well as their personal stories. Thank you Helen (Jarvis) Reynolds, Tony Fernandez, Jasmine Bryant, Yvette Quinones, Chris Malinowski, Tracy McCarthy, David Hogan, and anyone else who has shared their ideas along the way. You were all instrumental in bringing this book to life, and I appreciate each one of you. Yvette, you shared your self-care practices along with a very personal story so eloquently, that I was inspired to end one of my chapters with your words. Thank you for your contribution. This book has been in the making for so long, that there is a possibility I may have forgotten someone. If this is the case, please accept my humble apologies, as I am always grateful for the many people who enrich my life, and therefore have influenced this book.

I would like to express my appreciation to all whom I have come into contact with during my career in public education. This has been the platform for doing my work, for the evolvement of myself in many ways, and ultimately, the inspiration for this book. Thank you to my coworkers, students, and any and all who have influenced and supported me in this field through the years.

I would like to offer a special thank you to my family: for your love, support, and encouragement through the years. I wouldn't be who I am without all of you. Dad, thank you for always being in my corner. Thank you for teaching by example, not only how to treat others, but how to bask in life's simple pleasures. Mom, thank you for your continued love and support. You have always modeled generosity, even when you have had little from which to give. To both Mom and Dad, my phone chats with each of you always make my day brighter, and I am well aware of what a blessing you both are to me. Thank you for getting along with each other even though you are no longer together. You two, as well as my entire extended family, have taught me that it is possible to let bygones be bygones, and still remain a family, despite the many changes the years inevitably bring.

My final expression of gratitude is for my two wonderful children, each amazing in their own ways. Naturally, they are heavily sprinkled throughout this book, for they are my life and my heart. To my beautiful, talented Jasmine, thank you for sharing your self-care ideas and interesting perspectives. I was honored to include them in this work. To my handsome, compassionate son Zachary, thank you for your continued kindness, appreciation, and encouragement. I can't tell you how much it meant to me each time you saw me writing and said, "You've got this!" Jaz and Zach, I love you both more than words could express, and I feel truly blessed to be your mom.

Other titles from Higher Ground Books & Media:

Fill Your Cup Daily Journal by Deborah Armstrong Bryant

Raven Transcending Fear by Terri Kozlowski

The Power of Knowing by Jean Walters

Forgiven and Not Forgotten by Terra Kern

Through the Sliver of a Frosted Window by Robin Melet

Breaking the Cycle by Willie Deeanjlo White

Healing in God's Power by Yvonne Green

Chronicles of a Spiritual Journey by Stephen Shepherd

The Real Prison Diaries by Judy Frisby

The Words of My Father by Mark Nemetz

The Bottom of This by Tramaine Hannah

Add these titles to your collection today!

http://www.highergroundbooksandmedia.com/shop

HIGHER GROUND BOOKS & MEDIA IS

AN INDEPENDENT PUBLISHER

Do you have a story to tell?

Higher Ground Books & Media is an independent Christian-based publisher specializing in stories of triumph! Our purpose is to empower, inspire, and educate through the sharing of personal experiences. We are always looking for great, new stories to add to our collection. If you're looking for a publisher, get in touch with us today!

Please be sure to visit our website for our submission guidelines.

http://www.highergroundbooksandmedia.com/submission-guidelines

HGBM SERVICES IS OUR CONSULTING FIRM

AUTHOR SERVICES

HGBM Services offers a variety of writing and coaching services for aspiring authors! We can help with editing, manuscript critiques, self-publishing, and much more! Get in touch today to see how we can help you make your dream of becoming an author a reality!

*****

We also offer social media marketing services for authors, small businesses, and non-profit organizations. Let us help you get the word out about your book, your projects, and your mission. We offer great rates, quality promos, consistent communication, and a personal touch!

http://www.highergroundbooksandmedia.com/editing-writing-services

132

Need Bulk Copies?

If you would like to order bulk copies of this book or any other title at Higher Ground Books & Media, please contact us at highergroundbooksandmedia@gmail.com.

We offer discounts for purchases of 20 or more copies. Excellent for small groups, book clubs, classrooms, etc.

Get in touch today and get a set of great stories for your students or group members.

Made in the USA
Monee, IL
06 April 2023

31469562R00077